The
Quotable
Runner

Great Moments
of Wisdom,
Inspiration,
Wrongheadedness,
and Humor

Edited by Mark Will-Weber

BREAKAWAY BOOKS
HALCOTTSVILLE, N EW YORK

THE QUOTABLE RUNNER:
Great Moments of Wisdom, Inspiration, Wrongheadedness, and Humor

Compilation copyright © 1995, 2001 by Mark Will-Weber
Introduction and chapter essays copyright © 1995, 2001 by Mark Will-Weber
Revised and updated in 2001 for the first paperback edition.

Photos by Victor Sailer © Photo Run, except where otherwise noted.

ISBN: 978-1-891369-26-1

Published by:
BREAKAWAY BOOKS
P.O. Box 24
Halcottsville, NY 12438
(800) 548-4348
www.breakawaybooks.com

Breakaway Books are distributed by:
Consortium Book Sales & Distribution

10   9   8   7   6

For my father, who encouraged me to run; for my mother, who encouraged me to write; and for my wife, Sally (and daughter Jordy), who have lent their support as I have pursued both passions.

ACKNOWLEDGMENTS

To acknowledge the people who contributed to this book would be to recognize decades of runners, coaches and journalists of our sport. I cannot even try—even the quotes in this book cannot serve as complete acknowledgement, since I'm aware that some pretty good stuff (for one reason or another, as in any project) landed on the cutting room floor.

But closer to home, and high on the list, a most special thanks to:

Garth Battista, publisher and editor at feisty Breakaway Books, who believed in this project from start to finish; Brian Lenton of Australia, who unselfishly shared lots of the best stuff from his excellent books *Through The Tape* and *Off The Record*—including some five-star quotes from Chris Wardlaw, Kenny Moore, Ron Clarke, Herb Elliott, Albie Thomas and others; Peter Gambaccini, who wrote the excellent text for *The New York City Marathon— Twenty Five Years*, and passed on some beautiful Big Apple bites for *The Quotable Runner*; Carla Thomas, who placed her purposeful shoulder to the wheel in the late miles; Victor Sailer, racing photographer extraordinare, who charged over the hill like the U.S. Cavalry when the cry went forth for art; Amby Burfoot, executive editor of

Runner's World and 1968 Boston Marathon champ, who once said to me: "You've got the book sitting in your computer. Why don't you just *do* it . . . "; and Adam Bean, my *Runner's World* colleague / training partner / sounding-board / friend, who pitched in with editing assistance and a helluva lot of encouragement.

Lastly, thanks to all the runners (especially the Greyhounds of Moravian College) whom I've been fortunate enough to coach over the last 15 years. The modest beginnings of this book began with my quest to inspire you.

In Memoriam

And in memory of Doug Byren, Steve Gable and Harry "Huck" Snyder—teammates and friends of my youth; gone, but not forgotten.

"The time you won your town the race / We chaired you through the market-place / Man and boy stood cheering by / And home we brought you shoulder-high . . ."

—M. W. W., Bethlehem, Pennsylvania

CONTENTS

Introduction
BY MARK WILL-WEBER

Compiling a book of quotations is a bit like prospecting. For long, unrewarded hours you sift through the silt, murk, and bottom mud which comprise the great body of sports literature and journalism—all for that rare nugget of gold.

I began work on *The Quotable Runner* without actually realizing that I was doing it. (I highly recommend this method for any lengthy task if you can arrange it.) The first few hundred quotations that I gathered were used at the bottom of race results, in batches of five or six quotes per race, which I passed on to the cross-country runners at Moravian College in Bethlehem, Pennsylvania. As their coach, I thought it might be a fun way to jazz up the results sheets and inspire the runners to train with diligence and a new spark. Maybe a line from Zatopek, Nurmi, or Benoit would ignite a dream.

And so I collected some of these snippets of wisdom, humor and inspiration for approximately six years until one day I thought: "Hey, these might be of interest to other runners. . . . Why not bring them together in one collection?" (Someone of superior intellect might have thought of this angle much sooner. I confess, I am a slow learner.)

At any event, I then made a conscious surge to the front—running down quotes in magazines, books, newspapers and coaches' bulletin boards. My intent was to inspire and entertain other runners—young runners like those on my team, and not-so-young runners like those with whom I've trained and raced for the last 26 years.

Perhaps a more subtle (and pleasantly surprising) discovery was that *The Quotable Runner*—when considered in full—reflects the history, the spirit, and the art of our sport. Consider each specific quote as a colorful piece of tile, which, when all brought together, create a mosaic.

As for the accompanying essays that kick off each chapter, they encouraged me to take a nostalgic glance back into some of my own running experiences. I wanted to remember how the freshly-cut grass smelled that first August evening when I showed up for high school cross-country practice; the sound those long dagger spikes made on the old cinder tracks; and even that helpless feeling of a marathon unraveling at mile 19 or 20.

Gathering quotes is an interpretive art—and certainly not an exact science. For example, there's a quote in this book from Emil Zatopek concerning the marathon (The one I used begins like this: "We are different, in essence, from other men . . .") that I've seen used in four or five slightly different ways. So, either Zatopek used the quotation several times (changing several words here and there), or a "whisper-down-the-lane" effect took place—with the occasional variation occurring as the quote got "passed on" and used by other writers after its initial utterance.

Few books, if any, get by without the occasional "gremlin" creeping in to sabotage the effort. Consider the "slog and drudge" quote (attributed to English distance runner and former 10,000-meter world record holder David Bedford) that I used in the Training chapter. Just prior to the 1995 Boston Marathon I was introduced to Bedford in a Beantown bar. I told him that I was using the "slog and drudge" quote in the book. Bedford, who has a reputation for preferring beer to any journalist he's ever met, snarled (in good-natured jest, I think): "I never bloody said that!" I told Bedford I was still going to use the quote. It sure *sounded* like something Bedford would have said. And I had no reason to question my source.

But, since we found ourselves at the bar together, why not give me another quote for the book? Something profound and reflective on his years of racing, perhaps?

"All roit," the ever-irascible Bedford replied, "I'll give you a quote: 'It's all fun until you [expletive deleted] lose!'"

Therefore, the "slog and drudge" quote is only "attributed to," meaning, Bedford officially disowns it—despite its Shakespearean qualities. But the second quote I heard straight from the horse's mouth.

Finally, I have willfully concentrated on the middle and long distances in this book. I do not apologize for this. The odd hurdler or sprinter sneaks in here and there, but I never fully understood guys who thought a half dozen 30-meter starts out of the blocks constituted a workout. Then again, if God had seen fit to bless me with a bit more fast-twitch muscle fiber, this book might be called *Quotations from the Very Quick*. Or perhaps it would not be at all. Distance runners, admittedly, have lots of time to think.

The Starting Line: Great Beginnings

I see you stand like greyhounds in the slips,
straining upon the start.

—Shakespeare, *Henry V*

THE STARTING LINE

Someone once asked a highly respected Swedish sports physiologist what was the most crucial criterion for becoming an Olympic champion. The scientist issued a wry reply: "Choosing the right parents."

There is more than a little truth to that statement. Genetics tend to tip the athletic scale in one direction or another: therefore, we'll never see Charles Barkley ride the winning thoroughbred in the Kentucky Derby. Conversely, the best jockey at Churchill Downs will be driving the lane in an NBA final about the same time that the Devils (*not* the hockey franchise) are hosting the Stanley Cup.

And so, is it simply that the great runners are born on the very slopes of Mount Olympus, and from there rapidly ascend to even greater heights? Not necessarily. Long-distance running has traditionally reflected the notion that hard work, tough-mindedness and smart training and racing strategies can (if only to a certain extent) offset the natural ability factors. Most top runners begin much the same way we all do: by accident, by fending off uncertainties and self-doubt, by clinging to bits of inspiration and example from those that have run before them. They begin because they can't smash a baseline backhand or throw a wicked curveball; because they wanted to beat their big brother; because they discovered the incomparable exhilaration of a few well-run miles; or because some moron on the fifth grade playground babbled: "Girls can't play sports. . . ." The world class ones just find themselves on a higher level once all the *trying* is done.

In his book, *A Clean Pair of Heels*, Murray Halberg of New Zealand wrote: "I had always imagined an Olympic champion was something more than a mere mortal, in fact, a god. Now I knew he was just a human being." Halberg's conclusion came after he—a man whose left arm was rendered virtually useless by an injury incurred while playing rugby at age 17—won the 5000-meter gold medal in Rome.

In a world that says "You're too tired" and "You don't have time" and "Only money matters," running makes us Brothers and Sisters of the road. That's why running is not just about burning calories. That's why running is about more than just stress release, or honing a heart that pounds better than a kettle drum. If health is your main goal, you can achieve that on a stationary bike watching "Fantasy Island" re-runs.

Running is *real* and relatively simple—but it ain't easy. It's a challenge. It takes work. It takes commitment. You have to get out of bed, get out the door, down the street. You have to risk getting cold, wet, or too hot. Maybe whack some over-zealous hound on the snout—or "Hot Rod Harry" on the hood—every now and again. And, of course, you have to take your very first run.

"   "

"One day the factory sports coach, who was very strict, pointed at four boys, including me, and ordered us to run in a race. I protested that I was weak and not fit to run, but the coach sent me for a physical examination and the doctor said that I was perfectly well. So I had to run, and when I got started I felt I wanted to win. But I only came in second. That was the way it started."

—**Emil Zatopek**, Czechoslovakian Olympic great

◆

"Great people and great athletes realize early in their lives their destiny, and accept it. Even if they do not consciously realize the how, the where, the what."

—**Percy Cerutty**

◆

"If you want to become the best runner you can be, start now. Don't spend the rest of your life wondering if you can do it."

—**Priscilla Welch,** masters marathon great

◆

"When I first started running, I was so embarrassed, I'd walk when cars passed me. I'd pretend I was looking at the flowers."

—**Joan Benoit Samuelson**

◆

"It was a big ego trip. All the kids I hung around with were impressed. But then I took about a five year layoff."

—**Don Kardong** on a 4-mile run to his
grandmother's house when he was 10 years old

◆

"I ran to get a letter jacket, a girlfriend. I ran because I was cut from the basketball and baseball teams. I ran to be accepted, to be a part of a group."

—Jim Ryun

"He was a pretty good guitar player. He used to play with a band until I told him he would have to choose between guitar and track. He couldn't do both and be a four-minute miler."

—Fred Dwyer, Marty Liquori's high school coach

"My parents had a certain idea of what they wanted their 'little girl' to be and it did not include a budding track star."   **—Grete Waitz**

"It was cold and snowy that day, and I didn't have any running shoes."

—Steve Jones, on his first run in Barry, Wales

"When I was small I was very naughty and my father chased me with his belt to give me a thrashing. Maybe that was how I got accustomed to running."

— **Fermin Cacho**, 1992 Olympic 1500 champion

◆

"At our East German youth festivals one year, I won 10 gold medals and one silver. And my father was angry about the silver."

— **Uta Pippig**

◆

"I'd had operations on both feet at the age of 13 to correct some bone deformities and I'd been in plaster for six months, and when the plaster came off, I had to learn to walk and run properly. A year later I joined the running club, doing the sprints."

— **Anne Audain**, New Zealand

◆

"He was too small for football and he got tired of sitting on the bench all the time."

— **Ray Prefontaine**, on how his son Steve got started in running

◆

"It was back in 1901, at the age of twenty-one, when I first became interested in distance running. While attending a smoker at the University of Vermont to pep up enthusiasm for a football game, one of the speakers—a Professor Stetson of the German Department—urged all men to try different sports they could be a champion at. At once I wondered what I could be tops at. . . . By a process of elimination, I went out for cross-country."

—**Clarence DeMar** (who went on to win seven Boston Marathons)

"I wanted to be a hurdler or something. But when we had tryouts, I was so afraid to try out that I just refused, kind of hung in the back of the crowd hoping I wouldn't get noticed. The last event was the mile. And the coaches said: 'Porter hasn't done anything yet.' So there I was committed; enter Pat Porter, distance runner."

—**Pat Porter**

"When I went up to Oxford, I wanted to take part in sport. I was too light for rowing, and I wasn't skilled enough for rugby. But I knew I could run."

—**Sir Roger Bannister**

"I took up running simply to improve my fitness for rugby, which was my main sport. . . . I started running longer races, even marathons, the day after playing rugby, which didn't do my times much good. When I went to college I started playing less, partly because there were so many idiots playing the game, and I got more fearful of a major injury."

> —**Steve Brace,** who won the Berlin Marathon in 1991 in 2:10:57

"When I was 12 or 13, the first day I went out, there was a mile cross country race on and they said, 'You can't compete, you're too young,' because it was a race with 18-year-olds and like that, and I cried, literally cried, because they wouldn't let me run the race. So they said, 'Okay,' and I beat all these guys who were 18 and over, because I wanted to accept the challenge."

> —**Eamonn Coghlan**

"When I was fifteen, Clarke was running the world records and I used to imagine I was him. We lived on a very dark street in the inner Melbourne suburb of Prahran and if I had to get the milk or something at night

I'd charge out the front gate. Suddenly I'd be Clarkey tearing away and surging. I was very impressionable."

—**Chris Wardlaw,** Australian Olympic marathoner

◆

"We used to have field days there. That's where I ran my first race. I beat a boy and he pushed me down. I guess that's how it all started."

—**Joan Benoit Samuelson,** pointing out the
Cottage Farms School, Maine, to a visitor

◆

"At my school, I was timekeeper. It was my responsibility to make sure the other students were on time. So it was important that I arrived always first."

—**Ibrahim Hussein,** who ran several miles to
school each day as a boy in Kenya

◆

"I made the school team, and when I won in a match against another school it was the greatest moment of my life—even greater than the European titles. In those school races, I always ran my legs off. There were girls watching and I wanted to impress them. I was foaming and vomiting, but I won."

—**Juha Väätäinen,** Finland

"I wasn't too conscious of it then, but I know my going into running with a vengeance was to have something clear, definable and precise. Distances are distances and a watch is a watch. You're not depending on some unpredictable impression you're making on a girl. I remember there was a girl I wanted to impress and she was interested in a guy who pole vaulted and ran the mile. I was totally hopeless at the pole vault but at least I thought I could peg him over a mile. I tried and tried but I never did beat him in junior high. By then I was pretty well stuck into running for its own sake. The connection with the ferment of adolescence is a vital one for many runners. It certainly was for me."
　　—Kenny Moore

◆

"Running is the classical road to self-consciousness, self-awareness and self-reliance. Independence is the outstanding characteristic of the runner. He learns the harsh reality of his physical and mental limitations when he runs. He learns that personal commitment, sacrifice and determination are his only means to betterment. Runners only get promoted through self-conquest."
　　—Noel Carroll

"I spent most of my time playing soccer. I was a goal-keeper and I was good at it. But I started to run after I began winning a lot of school races."

— **Hicham El Gerrouj,** Moroccan star who set the
WR for the mile, 3:43.13, in July 1999

◆

"When I was 14 or 15, my brother tried to encourage me by giving me a pair of running shoes. But I threw them away because I was so used to running with bare feet and they were too heavy."

— **Haile Gebrselassie,** Ethiopian distance great

◆

"I lost my first race at school and I was so jealous when the winner received a puppet that I said to myself, 'I will carry on until I win a puppet.' "

— **Svetlana Masterkova,** WR holder in the
women's mile (4:12.56) and Olympic great

Voices from the Midpack
(And Elsewhere)

Talk to me not
of time and place;
I owe I'm happy
in the chase.

—**Shakespeare**, Epistle to David Garrick, Esq.

VOICES FROM THE MIDPACK
(And Elsewhere)

I was tempted to include a quote from my dentist, Karl Glassman, in this chapter, but there were a couple of downsides to it. First, everybody would say, "Who the hell is Karl Glassman?" (Well, I just told you . . .) And, second, Karl's quote is a simple one, and it loses some of its punch on paper, because when Karl says, "I used to be a fat dentist!" (that's the quote), his smile usually stretches out as wide as a finish line banner.

Like a number of late-comers to the sport, Karl's enthusiasm for running has surpassed many of those who raced in high school or college. We are talking about a guy here who has a framed *Chariots of Fire* movie poster facing one of his dental chairs. A guy who ran as part of a relay with a Maccabian Games torch from JFK Airport in New York to Allentown, Pennsylvania. A guy who wants to know the details of your latest half-marathon effort, while you have dental tools, pieces of cotton, and a couple of suction hoses crammed in your mouth.

I've always marveled at Karl's enthusiasm for running and he's always exemplified a certain theory that I have about our sport of long-distance running: that is, in running (like religion), it's the converts who are likely to exhibit the most zeal. And for that reason, the continuing influx of average beginning runners will always be the lifeblood of this sport.

What about non-runners—i.e., the voices from the sideline? As a young newspaper reporter, I once interviewed George V. Higgins, an accomplished Boston author of some twenty novels. I just happened to be in town for the marathon, of course, to which Higgins—in all seriousness, I think—asked me: "Do you guys puke in the street after you run that thing, or what?"

Well, today's non-runner could *conceivably* be a beginning runner somewhere down the road. But even if they are not likely to lace on a pair of running shoes in the next century, that's okay. Non-runners can add some counterbalance to our fanaticism. Show me a real runner and I will show you someone who has, at least on occasion, become too wrapped up in the sport. For example, a sure sign is when you have absolutely no clue who the state governor is—or that your tenth wedding anniversary is tomorrow—but you can rattle off each and every 400-split from some guy's latest 10,000-meter record assault staged at Bislett Stadium in Oslo, Norway.

Besides, if it wasn't for non-runners, it'd be that much harder to get a seat in the non-smoking section of your favorite restaurant. Or something like that.

" "

1. THE MIDPACK ATTACK

"In running, it doesn't matter whether you come in first, in the middle of the pack or last. You can say, 'I have finished.' There is a lot of satisfaction in that."
—**Fred Lebow**

◆

"The average American takes twenty years to get out of condition and he wants to get back in condition in twenty days—and you just can't do it."
—**Ken Cooper, M. D.**

◆

"There is no doubt that 'Sport For All' is a 20th-century movement of real significance. Other mass movements have oppressed where they intended to liberate. This movement liberates because it has an essentially individual basis. The choice of speed, route, distance or company is entirely yours."

—Sir Roger Bannister

◆

"I get more gratification out of getting some obese person who had a heart attack running around and enjoying life within a year. I get more gratification from that than putting a person in the Olympic Games. The Olympic athlete probably doesn't appreciate what you've done, but the other guy does. I think it's really rewarding."

—Arthur Lydiard

◆

"The difference between a jogger and a runner is an entry blank."

—Dr. George Sheehan

◆

"In track, people like you are in the stands. In road racing, you're on the course with me at the same time, running the same hills, taking the same water. You can relate to me. And I can relate to you."
   —**Rod Dixon**

◆

"You know who I look up to? I look up to the five-minute milers. Because they don't get any of the good things I get. They're out there running just as hard. They're the guys with guts, the guys with a lot of inner determination."
   —**Mark Belger**, former Villanova star, 1971

◆

"Start slowly, then taper off."
   —**Walt Stack**, racing advice

◆

"The 'talk test' was the greatest news I'd heard since I found out it was okay to eat pasta: If you're out of breath, slow down. What a great deal!"
   —**George** "Norm from 'Cheers'" **Wendt**, actor

◆

"I felt great and I didn't barf or anything."
> — **Anonymous** woman finisher at the 1994
> Bloomsday Run

◆

"We wondered if there would be paddy wagons along the way to pick us up—like pooper-scoopers."
> —**Judy Driggers**, back-of-the-pack finisher in the
> Charleston Bridge Run 10-K, 1994

◆

"It was hard to find a pool when I was modeling in New York, so I took up running."
> —**Kim Alexis**, supermodel and marathoner

◆

"I use running to gain energy. Laurence Olivier's advice to young actors was to gain physical strength, and it's the same advice I would give to young writers. If you're going to succeed in a very, very competitive, difficult profession, you'd better be fit."
> —**Israel Horovitz**, playwright

◆

"I don't know how the creative process works, but it always seems, as I'm running . . . that thoughts start coming in; sentences start coming in."
— **Robert A. Caro**, biographer

◆

"To be a good mayor or a good politician, you need to feel good about yourself. You have to believe in yourself and running certainly helps that. I feel good. I feel healthy. Because I feel good, I think I have energy to spread around, to take care of my responsibility as mayor."
— **Jim Scheibel**, Mayor of St. Paul,
2:40 marathon PR

◆

"Distance running to a professional athlete in my day was five laps around the field. And you stopped each lap to take your pulse."
— **Lynn Swann**, former Pittsburgh Steeler

◆

"My feeling is that any day I am too busy to run is a day that I am too busy."
— **John Bryant**, deputy editor of the London
Times, 1994

"I always go for a run the morning of the NFL draft. If I can't go extra long, then I go extra hard. It's the same the morning of a game. If I let up, then I feel something will go wrong. I don't know why—it's kind of silly—but I've always felt that way."

> —**Bobby Beathard,** General Manager, San Diego
> Chargers, 2:46 PR for the marathon

◆

"Sometimes people will say to me, 'Oprah's got it easy because she has a personal chef and a personal trainer.' But that's baloney. No one can run for you. She was on the track every morning. She worked herself as hard as any athlete I've seen. She deserved the results she achieved."

> —**Bob Greene,** Oprah Winfrey's personal trainer,
> after she finished the Marine Corps Marathon

◆

"Running is the greatest metaphor for life, because you get out of it what you put into it."

> —**Oprah Winfrey**

◆

"I like running because it's a challenge. If you run hard, there's the pain—and you've got to work your way *through* the pain. You know, lately it seems all you hear is 'Don't overdo it' and 'Don't push yourself.' Well, I think that's a lot of bull. If you push the human body, it will respond."

—**Bob Clarke**, Philadelphia Flyers general
manager, NHL Hall of Famer

◆

"I have had only one problem with my running, and that was in prison. I was in nine different prisons, and in one of the prisons we could only run in the yard. The yard—it was five laps to the mile roughly—was hard-packed earth. It was almost like concrete and I was wearing those shoes which had no shock absorption at all. There was a rule that you could only run in one direction, the reason being if people ran in different directions, the guards thought they might bump into each other and start a riot. So here we were all running in one direction. I woke up one morning and I couldn't move my left hip. . . . The only problem I see with long distance running when you get to be my age is something starts to wear. In my case, it was the hip . . . Hell, I could run the marathon but I don't know what I'd do with the hip. I'd have to bring it along in a wheelbarrow."

>   —**G. Gordon Liddy,** Watergate burglar, radio talk
>   show host

◆

"In running, if I get tired, I'll stop; in boxing, if you get tired and stop; you'll get murdered."

>   —**Floyd Patterson,** former world heavyweight
>   champ prior to running the NYC Marathon

◆

"When I did this three years ago, it was like death. When I did it last year, it was like near death. This year, it was just really hard."

>   —Wheelchair racer **John Howie**'s description of
>   his three Charlotte Observer 10-K races, 1993

◆

"I act my age better than she does. And I wash the dishes."

>   —**Carl Lindgren,** Mavis Lingren's husband, after
>   Mavis completed the 1986 New York
>   Marathon at age 86

"Hunker down, keep your eyes fixed ahead, and run like hell."

> —**Paul Spangler**, advice to Sister Marion Irvine before a race. Spangler set 85 national age group records prior to his death at 95.

◆

"It's elevating and humbling at the same time. Running along a beach at sunrise with no other footprints in the sand, you realize the vastness of creation, your own insignificant space in the plan, how tiny you really are, your own creatureliness and how much you owe to the supreme body, the God that brought all this beauty and harmony into being."

> —**Sister Marion Irvine**, 2:51 PR and 1984 U.S. Olympic Marathon Trials qualifier

◆

"You can listen to the stream run. You can listen to the birds. Music is my life, but running allows me to appreciate the music of the outdoors."

> —**Gail Williams**, hornplayer

◆

"Running helps me stay on an even keel and in an optimistic frame of mind."

　　—**Bill Clinton**, President of the United States

◆

"Running helps me be more productive. . . . I'll be running until I'm a little old lady."

　　—**Claudine Schneider**, Congresswoman

◆

"I think the most common reason people don't run is that they are afraid other people might laugh at them."

　　—**Senator William Proxmire**, pre-running boom

◆

"I was too embarrassed to be another fat guy in new running shoes and sweats, so we'd go out at night with a flashlight. . . . I found out that runners weren't judgmental."

　　—**George "Norm" Wendt**, actor

◆

"I tend to keep the old ones [running shoes]. I just can't throw them out. . . . I've got a pair of running shoes that I wore in Africa. It was a rainy, nasty day. After the run, I propped the shoes on some rocks by our campfire, and they got kind of burned. Every time I look at these burned shoes, I think about that trip in Africa, so I don't want to throw them out."

—**Tom Brokaw**, NBC news anchorman

"Someone lent us a cottage in Hartsfordshire. I was sitting in a sort of parlor there one day, writing. And suddenly I saw someone run past the window, along the lane outside. With shorts on, white shirt and so on. And it seemed to me such an unusual image . . . that I wrote down at the top of a sheet of paper, 'the loneliness of the long-distance runner.' I didn't know where he had come from, I didn't know where he was going. He was simply a sort of . . . vision, floating by the window. And I put the line away, I thought I was going to write a poem with this sort of line in it. It seemed rather a nice line."

—**Alan Sillitoe,** author of *The Loneliness of the Long-Distance Runner*

"I love running cross-country, especially where I live in Northern California. . . . You come up a hill and see two deer going, 'What the hell is he doing?' On a track, I feel like a hamster."

—**Robin Williams**, film star / comic

2. SIDELINE ASIDES
(Detractors and Reactors)

"It must be spring; the saps are running."
>—derogatory remark popular with non-runners
>in the early years of the Boston Marathon

"It is the spectacle of foolish people racing around town in their underwear, the familiar Underwear Nightmare come true."
>—*Washington Star*, on running

"If the Lord had meant for man to run, he'd have given him four legs or at least made him late for a bus."
>—**Red Smith**, sportswriter

◆

"I've never seen a computer jogging."
>—**Frank Layden,** basketball coach, on why
>computers are smarter than people

◆

"I believe that the good Lord gave us a finite number of heartbeats and I'm damned if I'm going to use up mine running up and down a street."

>—**Neil Armstrong**, astronaut

◆

"All that running and exercise can do for you is make you healthy."

>—**Denny McLain**, two-time Cy Young award
>winner for the Detroit Tigers

◆

"Hell, no. When I die I want to be sick."

>—**Abe Lemons**, basketball coach, when asked
>why he didn't jog

◆

"It's unnatural for people to run around city streets unless they are thieves or victims. It makes people nervous to see someone running. I know that when I see someone running on my street, my instincts tell me to let the dog out after him."

>—**Mike Royko**, newspaper columnist

◆

Coaches

"Then would begin Stephen's run around the park. Mike Flynn would stand at the gate near the railway station, watch in hand, while Stephen ran around the track in the style Mike Flynn favoured, his head high lifted, his knees well lifted and his hands held straight down by his sides. When the morning practice was over the trainer would make his comments and sometimes illustrate them by shuffling along for a yard or so comically in an old pair of blue canvas shoes. . . .Though he had heard his father say that Mike Flynn had put some of the best runners of modern times through his hands Stephen often glanced at his trainer's flabby stubble-covered face, as it bent over the long stained fingers through which he rolled his cigarette, and with pity at the mild lustreless blue eyes."

—**James Joyce**, *Portrait of the Artist as a Young Man*

COACHES

I have this theory that people who are a pain in the butt to their coaches will one day themselves be condemned to coach. I put forth this proposition only partly in jest, as I find myself in my 15th year of coaching.

My definition of a great distance running coach would be this: someone who helps you improve but leaves something "in the bank," and also instills love of the sport as you move on. Plus, one hopes, someone who teaches you something about life in the process.

I think of Lydiard, saying that the next Olympic champion lives in your neighborhood . . . Of Mussabini, banned from the stadium in Paris, punching his jubilant fist through a straw hat after Abrahams won the 100 meters . . . Of Haikkola, stern before Viren in the wilds of Lapland, saying: "We will no longer speak about the leg . . . " Of Jumbo Elliott, dapper and confident, smiling grand and Irish in the old splintery stands at Penn, producing generations of great distance runners. I think of Nakamura, trudging to the trout stream, head bowed, ancestors peering down from Heaven . . . Of Bowerman, wrecking his wife's waffle iron to make soles for his runners. I think of Cerutty—gaunt as a poor man's scarecrow—hammering his sun-baked, bony frame round the red, dusty track, shaking a leathery fist at his athletes, eyes popping from his weathered face, saying: "You may run faster tomorrow, but you won't run any bloody harder!"

My first real distance running coach was Jim Gulick at North Penn High School, Lansdale, Pennsylvania. He was a great coach who followed in the footsteps of a great coach, Jim Crawford Sr. I realize most runners reflect glowingly about their high school coaches, but they *were* great coaches in terms of both sport and life, as was my college coach, Dick DeSchriver at East Stroudsburg University. They met and exceeded all the criteria listed above.

As I reflect on my experiences as a high school and college runner, I'm painfully aware that I lacked the maturity to take full advantage of all that I might have learned from my coaches. Coach Gulick had a deep, booming voice, and to a skinny 17-year-old boy trying to hone some sort of self-image from that mess we term adolescence, his voice was resoundingly god-like—like Zeus or Thor. The voice seemed all the more powerful because he rarely used it.

In my senior year (back from a recent bout with mono), I found myself in the middle of a two-mile race against Wissahickon. Brad Perry, an excellent runner for Wissy, was pulling away from me on the backstretch. Coach Gulick's voice reverberated off the stands, across the infield, over the track: "Don't take pity on yourself, Mark Weber!!"

And I did try to dig a little deeper (or at least I think I did), but it was like one of those bad dreams where you just can't go any faster and everyone floats by while you flail your arms and legs. I never closed the gap. Maybe I held on for third, salvaged a fourth.

But years later, trying to persevere beyond the wall in some marathon or reach down for one last lung-burning burst in a cross-country race, I was always able to hear Gulick's voice: "Don't take pity on yourself, Mark Weber!" Once I remember thinking to myself: "Jesus, thirty-five years old and you're still reacting to that phrase like it's some conditioned response."

It was not a negative. More often than not, that thought alone would get me through what the British runners are fond of calling "a bad patch." Sometimes (rarely), I could actually ignite some kind of rally with it, win a local road race, nail down an elusive PR, make the other guy "earn it." In effect, do what I couldn't do that day when Perry pulled away from me in that high school race.

More frequently, Jim Gulick's words were simply something that I could cling to when the race wasn't going well, like pieces of driftwood in the aftermath of a shipwreck, something that you could grasp, pull to yourself and reach shore and safety. Yes, that was it. Something that could get you back to where you could start over again.

" "

COACH: What are yer legs?
ARCHIE HAMILTON: Steel springs.
COACH: What are they gonna do?
ARCHIE: Hurl me down the track!
COACH: How fast can ya run?
ARCHIE: Fast as a leopard!
COACH: How fast *are* ya gonna run?
ARCHIE: Fast as a leopard!
COACH: Well, all right, leopard, let's see ya do it then!
    —Opening lines from the movie *Gallipoli*

"You must always realize one thing. In every little village in the world there are great potential champions who only need motivation, development and good exercise evaluation."
—Arthur Lydiard

◆

"Like a father with a little bit of tyrant mixed in."
—Charlie Jenkins, Villanova runner and Olympian, describing Jumbo Elliott

◆

"He [Jumbo Elliott] forever sought 'the wolf,' the anchorman, the one who would make up the distance to the runner up ahead. His runners overachieved at times, became wolves to avoid his disappointment in them—or to avoid his occasional outbursts."
—Theodore J. Berry, M. D., in *Jumbo Elliott: Maker of Milers, Maker of Men*

◆

"To understand Cerutty you have to see him as a multi-faceted personality. He could be both charming and very abusive. He was extremely amusing and darn good company providing you weren't quarrelling with him"
—John Landy

"He [Percy Cerutty] was regarded as a ratbag and a crank and certainly an exhibitionist. I've been with him in public and wished I could climb under the seat and hide because of the things he said. Yet. . . I've known him to give away his last buck to athletes who were staying at Portsea. Perc was that sort of person and I've got lots of good words for him. Undoubtedly though, a real Jekyll and Hyde character."

—Albie Thomas

◆

"Bill Bowerman was, and is, and ever shall be a generous, ornery, profane, beatific, unyielding, antic, impenetrably complex Oregon original. As a freshman, I found him deeply disturbing. . . . Once he bet me a case of Nutrament that I couldn't break 2:00 for the 880 on a freezing Saturday morning. I ran with control, hitting the 440 in 60. I could feel myself accelerating in the last lap. Near the finish I knew I'd done it. I slowed and turned, gasping to hear the time. '2:00.3,' he said. 'Good try.' I leaped on him, screaming, made insane by outrage. He allowed me to wrestle the watch away from him. It read 1:56.6."

—Kenny Moore

◆

"Everybody and their mother knows you don't train hard on Friday, the day before a race. But a lot of runners will overtrain on Thursday if left on their own. . . .Thursday is the most dangerous day of the week."

  —Marty Stern, Villanova women's coach

◆

"If you want to tell something to an athlete, say it quickly and give no alternatives. This is a game of winning and losing. It is senseless to explain and explain."

  —Paavo Nurmi, advice to Lasse Viren's coach,
    Rolf Haikkola

◆

"Only think of two things—the report of the pistol and the tape. When you hear the one, just run like hell till you break the other."

  —Sam Mussabini, final advice to Harold
    Abrahams prior the 100 meters in Paris, 1924

◆

"It is true that speed kills. In distance running, it kills anyone who does not have it."

  —Brooks Johnson

"Act like a horse. Be dumb. Just run."
   —Jumbo Elliott

"God determines how fast you're going to run; I can help only with the mechanics."
   —Bill Bowerman

"In our business, son, we have a saying: 'You can't put in what God left out!'"
   —Sam Mussabini in *Chariots of Fire*

"I'm in heaven here. . . And my runners are my angels."
   —Joe Vigil on why he coached 30 years at Adams State in Alamosa, Colorado

"If a man coaches himself, then he has only himself to blame when he is beaten."
   —Sir Roger Bannister

"Coaches are okay, I guess, but I prefer to do things my own way."
   —Jack Foster

"Any distance coach is made famous by his runners as often as he makes the runners famous. It's world records and Olympic championships that draw attention to coaching methods and the men behind them. No matter how solidly based their methods might be, no one would have rushed to Igloi-type interval work if it hadn't been for Tabori's and Iharos' and Roszovolgyi's world marks. No one would have rushed to Cerutty's weight training and hill climbing if it hadn't been for Elliott. No one would have taken to the roads Lydiard-style if it hadn't been for Snell and Halberg. Success on a spectacular scale draws imitators."

—Joe Henderson

"Percy Cerutty coached him. However, Cerutty happened to be living in the same house which Elliott trained from. If Herb had been living at my grandmother's house he would still have been the best in the world."

—Ron Clarke

"Coaching an elite runner is something like driving an expensive car. The coach's main job is to steer."

—John Babington, Lynn Jennings' coach

"Most people need a coach to tell them to work hard; I need a coach to tell me to ease up. Sometimes I wish I had a coach to tell me, 'Okay, stop working, you've done enough,' because if you tell yourself that, you'll feel guilty and guilt is what keeps a lot of guys going after they should stop."
    —**Marty Liquori**, 1975

◆

"Several of my critics have said, 'Bowerman just tacks up a piece of paper in the locker room and turns his runners loose.' They're partially right. I do give the athletes a relatively free rein and for good reason. One of my principles is 'Don't overcoach.'"
    —**Bill Bowerman**

◆

"This habit of publicly committing their charges to highly demanding performances seems to be an unfortunate trait of most prominent coaches."
    —**Peter Snell**

◆

"We run every race together. We are the same person."
    —**Toshihiko Seko**, Japanese marathon great, on his
        deceased coach, Kiyoshi Nakamura

"Intelligent coaching is sometimes no coaching."
  —Marty Stern

◆

"I would have liked his advice and help at this moment, but I could not bring myself to ask him. It was as if now, at the end of my running career, I was being forced to admit that coaches were necessary after all."
  —Sir Roger Bannister, concerning Franz Stampfl, hours prior to the first sub-4 minute mile

◆

"I used to sit there and salivate waiting for Fred's letters, like Pavlov's dog. I'd get a letter, open it up, and devour his comments: 'Go, go, go! That's fantastic! You're going to be immortal!'"
  —Buddy Edelen, former world record holder in the marathon. Edelen trained in England and received his coaching advice from Fred Wilt via mail

◆

"Confidence is the most important quality in all athlete-coach relationships."
  —Franz Stampfl

"If the coach cannot do it, he cannot 'teach' it—only talk about it."
   —Percy Cerutty

"Well, no athlete respects a big, fat coach who's going to stand there and rest the watch on his stomach."
   —Arthur Lydiard

"The thinking must be done first, before training begins."
   —Peter Coe

◆

"When all the shouting is over and the senior partner has broken the record, the junior partner's reward comes from the satisfaction of a good job well done. Who could ask for more?"
   —Franz Stampfl

◆

"Every athlete has doubts. Elite runners in particular are insecure people. You need someone to affirm that what you are doing is right."
   —Lynn Jennings

"The primary reason to have a coach is to have some-body who can look at you and say, 'Man, you're lookin' good today.'"

> —**Jack Daniels,** exercise physiologist and coach of Div. III National champions State University of New York at Cortland

◆

"I would scold them or beat them when they were lazy or disobedient. But I only did it for their own good."

> —Chinese coach **Ma Junren,** on his former superteam of women runners dubbed "Ma's Army"

◆

"A coach can be like an oasis in the desert of a runner's lost enthusiasm."

> —**Ken Doherty**

◆

"Coaching is an art and I'm not going to let anyone change me."

> —**Marty Stern**

◆

"The coach's job is twenty percent technical and eighty percent inspirational."
—Franz Stampfl

◆

"He [his late Japanese coach, Nakamura] gave me a rose and told me it can be any color, but its thorns can also sting. It is so beautiful, yet so dangerous. My life depends on this one rose."
—Douglas Wakiihuri

◆

"I still bother with runners I call hamburgers. They're never going to run any record times. But they can fulfill their own potential."
—Bill Bowerman

◆

"Igloi compares his athletes with violin players preparing for an important concert. They repeat the same piece thousands of times. . . . One of Igloi's ex-runners compares him to Attila, who requested obedience from the Mongols."
—Arnd Kruger, *Igloi: Man and Method*

◆

"Mihaly Igloi came here from Hungary after the 1956 Olympics in Melbourne. He wouldn't appear at a clinic, because he thought somebody was trying to steal his ideas. Dale Ranson of North Carolina was with me on the NCAA rules committee, and he told me once: 'Igloi is going to be here, and I expect I'll learn a lot.' So after Igloi had been there for about six weeks, I called Dale and asked: 'So what did you find out from Igloi?' He said, 'I haven't found out a damn thing. He won't talk to me.' But Dale said, 'I've got an idea. I'm going up in the bell tower and watch him.' So he went up in the bell tower with binoculars and he sent me these notes on what Igloi had been doing. . . . So we added what Igloi called his sets—600, 400, 200—very productive, but I never got it from Igloi. I got it from Ranson."

—Bill Bowerman

◆

"A teacher is never too smart to learn from his pupils. But while runners differ, basic principles never change. So it's a matter of fitting your current practices to fit the event and the individual. See, what's good for you might not be worth a darn for the next guy."

—Bill Bowerman

"The key to distance coaching is to get the mixture right for each individual. I think most coaches in the world now know the basic ingredients of a runner's training program. What they have to do is to get to know their own athletes so well that they know the right recipe for them. It's a bit like making a Christmas cake: a question of individual taste."

—**Harry Wilson,** who coached Steve Ovett

◆

"People think Billy [Squires] is a little wacky, but I've never met anybody who knows as much about training as he does. I think of myself as a disciple of his. He really just took a little Lydiard and a little Bowerman like everyone else. But he added his own personality and insights. Most importantly, he taught me patience is the key to the development of a champion distance runner."

—**Bob Sevene,** who coached Joan Benoit

◆

"My strength comes from my coach. Just as Salazar runs with God, I run with coach Nakamura."

—**Toshihiko Seko**

◆

"As far as being a coach, it's always fascinated me. It's a greater responsibility than most people give it credit for because you're dealing with people."

—Steve Prefontaine

◆

"The only group lower than the athletes are the coaches."

> **—Bill Bowerman,** concerning politics of sport at the Olympic level

◆

"At the moment, with the way the sport is administered, I would rather farm than coach. . . . There would be frustrations that I don't want. Too much politics, too many demands."

> **—Ben Jipcho,** when asked if he would like to coach upon retiring from competition

◆

"Sometimes, when things have gone wrong, I feel sad and depressed. . . . I have a dream. When I retire, I want to become an inn-keeper. Occasionally, I hope this day will arrive tomorrow."

> **—Kari Sinkkonen**, Finnish coach

Eat, Drink, but Be Wary

Dost thou think because thou are virtuous there shall be no more cakes and ale?
—**Shakespeare,** *Twelfth Night*

EAT, DRINK, BUT BE WARY

Some runners (the wheat germ/bee pollen set) subscribe to the "body as temple" theory, and therefore "cakes and ale" would be considered high on the unwanted intruder list. I admire these runners for their virtue, but I cannot claim to be one of them.

Truth be told, the quote in this section that most represents my nutritional philosophy—if you can call it that—comes from John Parker's highly-acclaimed novel, *Once A Runner*. Parker says (proudly, I think) that it is the most frequently quoted line from the book: "If the furnace is hot enough, it will burn anything."

I most confess to some moderation in recent years. Once it seemed perfectly reasonable to polish off half a bag of Pepperidge Farm Irish Oatmeal cookies as a pre-race breakfast; now I'm more likely to opt for a plain bagel.

Back in the 1934, Princeton miler Bill "Bonny" Bonthron prepared for his match race against Glenn Cunningham of Kansas in an interesting fashion. Former Princeton team manager Peter Schwed related the story years later:

With senior theses out of the way, those final spring months at Princeton could be one of the most pleasant times in a person's life. Bonny was enjoying it to the hilt and, since the mile event wouldn't be run until about six o'clock that Saturday afternoon, decided that he need not forego his customary weekend program. Accordingly, he played 18 holes of golf in the morning and followed it with his regular hot weather luncheon—a *quart* of vanilla ice cream. Whether those were factors in his performance later that day or not, and Bill never said they were, he ran a ghastly race and Cunningham walked off with the mile run in record time.

Like training schedules, runners sometimes tend to embellish just how "bad"—or, less frequently, how "good"—their diets are. If you can believe half of what Don "Fruit Loops" Kardong says that he has eaten—or half of what other people have said Bill "mayonnaise-on-pizza" Rodgers has eaten, then you'd have to say those guys are potential medal winners in the hot-furnace division.

Pasta (despite some recent attacks that question just how

much nutritional punch the noodle wields) has traditionally been the darling of the pre-race meal. And yet, somebody recently told me that Carlos Lopes of Portugal wolfed down a large steak the evening prior to winning his marathon gold medal at the Los Angeles Olympics.

Beer, of course, is another story—and often a controversial one. More than a few runners—especially the pre-boom variety—have a fervent loyalty to the malt and barley suds, even to the point of claiming the brew offers "good carbos" (minimal, in fact) and "fluid replacement" (any form of alcohol can cause dehydration). Still, a couple of cold ones the night before a big race can help rock a nervous runner to sleep, right? Keep in mind that "a couple" only means "two."

Of course, some runners count better than others. In which case, moderation is probably the key word. Len Miller, who once coached miler Steve Scott, probably said it best: "Beer isn't going to help a runner but, in moderation, it won't hurt him either. If an athlete runs 75 to 120 miles a week, an occasional beer doesn't do a thing. He'll burn the calories right out of his body." Sounds suspiciously like the "hot furnace" theory to me.

" "

1. EATING

"The walk finished, you will be more than ready for breakfast. This should, nevertheless, be a fairly light meal. Two or three medium-boiled eggs, a little fish, perhaps, some dry toast, and, say, two cups of coffee in preference to tea. It is as well to take some oatmeal porridge now and then in order to supply the necessary building material for one's bones, which is to be found in oatmeal in greater quantity than in any other food with which I am acquainted."

> —**Alf Shrubb,** winner of 20 British distance
> titles between 1900 and 1904

◆

"My favorite diet was a glass of beer with some bread and cheese."

> —**Walter George,** English distance star, late 1800s

◆

"If the furnace is hot enough, it will burn anything."
　　　—**John Parker,** *Once a Runner*

◆

"If you run a hundred miles a week, you can eat anything you want—Why? Because (a) you'll burn all the calories you consume, (b) you deserve it, and (c) you'll be injured soon and back on a restricted diet anyway."
　　　—**Don Kardong**

◆

"There are three things worth living for: American luxury, Japanese women and Chinese food."
　　　—**Emil Zatopek,** joking

◆

"I wouldn't mind going over there if the food was okay. But I don't think I could stomach the turtle blood."
　　　—**Sonia O'Sullivan,** upon being asked if she'd
　　　　　consider training with the elite Chinese women

◆

"I will even try eating worms and caterpillar fungus. It might improve my jogging, and for sure it will improve my flossing."
　　　—**Scott Ostler,** *San Francisco Chronicle*

"There are some runners who can train in Kenya, but I cannot. When I am in Kenya, the people invite me to drink tea with them, or to share food with them. . . And in my country, it is considered a great insult to refuse such an invitation. . . . So you see, I always gain weight when I visit Kenya, and it's difficult to stay in top condition. But in the U.S., I can concentrate on my training—and people must call me before they can come visit."

> —**Ibrahim Hussein**, 3 time Boston Marathon champion

◆

"Pancakes. French toast. I don't eat very much compared to other runners. . . . When we used to go on trips, Jack [Bacheler] would get all my meals on the plane and then usually half of what I couldn't eat at night. Bacheler eats three times what I do."

> —**Frank Shorter**, 1975

◆

"If you feel like eating, eat. Let your body tell you what it wants." —**Joan Benoit Samuelson**

◆

"There's no such thing as a bad carbohydrate."
   —Don Kardong

◆

"It's like putting gas in your tank."
   —Nancy Clark, dietitian, on sports nutrition bars

◆

"All men and nations eat too much, and for this reason are not fit."
   —Paavo Nurmi, during a 1925 U.S. tour

◆

"One time I asked Clarence [DeMar] why the Orientals and Finns were such good runners and he said, 'They don't eat as much as we do.'"
   —Johnny A. "Old John" Kelley

◆

"Avoid any diet that discourages the use of hot fudge."
   —Don Kardong

◆

"Kardong's article was very dangerous and disgusting."
   —Reader's reaction to one of Don Kardong's "alternative" articles on diet

"It used to be that I'd eat to run—and the more I ran, the more I needed to eat. But now I run to eat. I love to eat."
—Tom Fleming

◆

"I eat whatever the guy who beat me in the last race ate."
—Alex Ratelle, masters runner

◆

"If you come to think of it, you never see deer, dogs and rabbits worrying about their menus and yet they run much faster than humans."
—Emil Zatopek

◆

"My whole teaching in one sentence is: 'Run slowly, run daily, drink moderately and don't eat like a pig.'"
—Dr. Ernest van Aaken, German coach

◆

"Without ice cream, there would be darkness and chaos."
—Don Kardong

◆

2. DRINKING (AND OTHER HABITS)

"In the face of the teetotallers I have recommended an occasional glass of old ale, and I am firmly of the impression that the athlete who indulges in an occasional glass of this will, other things being equal, derive greater benefits thereby than the man who preserves and adheres to a rigid teetotalism." —**Alf Shrubb**

◆

"Most athletic matches in England were arranged in the public houses [pubs] or sporting houses where the "fancy" or fans congregated. Some of these taverns became so closely associated with sporting activities that they constructed running tracks adjacent to the house."
—from *Runners & Walkers,* by John Cummings

◆

"The music is played in smoky bars at 11:30 or midnight. It would be easier if I were into symphonies."
—**Bob Kempainen** on his liking for postpunk, alternative music

◆

"All I want to do is drink beer and train like an animal."
—**Rod Dixon**

"As long as it's the other guy drinking it."

> —**Jim Fixx**, when asked if beer was good for marathoners

◆

"If I burn out in the next two or three years it won't be because of overtraining, it'll be because of attending too many raves."

> —**Shawn Found**

◆

"The running man who doesn't smoke is better off than the man who does. Smoking can never do one's wind any good, but I would not like to assert that one or two cigarettes, or say one pipe a day, will do a man any harm."

> —**Alf Shrubb**

◆

"I don't drink. I don't kiss girls. These things do an athlete in."

> —**Suleiman Nyambui**, distance star of the '80s

◆

"Never touch spirits of any kind. They are the worst thing an athlete can go for."

> —**Alf Shrubb**

"He's the hard-training, clean-living all-American boy and I'm the long-haired layabout who likes to stay up late every night and drink alcohol at parties."

> —**Nick Rose,** on the differences between himself and Craig Virgin back in 1976

◆

"Listen to your body. Do not be a blind and deaf tenant."

> —**Dr. George Sheehan**

◆

"The experts are always telling us to 'Listen to your body!' But if I listened to my body, I'd live on toffee pops and port wine. Don't tell me to listen to my body. . . . It's trying to turn me into a blob!"

> —**Roger Robinson,** New Zealand masters runner

◆

"Listen to my body? If I was listening to my body right now I would be home in bed eating a danish and reading the funnies."

> —Overheard at the 1991 San Antonio Marathon

◆

"Reindeer milk!"

> —**Lasse Viren,** on his "secret"

Training:
The Daily Sacrifice

Why dost thou run so many mile about?

—**Shakespeare,** *Richard III*

TRAINING
(The Daily Sacrifice)

There's a story that Murray Halberg, one of New Zealand's greatest runners (and the runner that coach Arthur Lydiard admired as the man who got the most out of himself), once won an alarm clock in a race. There was only one problem. The alarm clock was the second place prize. First place in that particular race had gone to Bruce Kidd of Canada. So every morning when the alarm clock jangled sometime before the sun came up, Halberg didn't need to look beyond his own night stand for an incentive to get up and train. And when his evening session was done, there was that bloody alarm clock—an instrument specifically designed to interrupt one's dreams—again, the key in the back of the intrusive contraption in need of constant winding.

Well, whether we are Murray Halberg or Murray the Jogger (who has his thirteen-day, once-round-the-block streak on the line), there isn't a whole lot of difference when you are staring down the gun-barrel of that big "zero" about to be etched in your training log.

Fear of slacking resides deep in the heart of every runner. When I was twenty-five, and traveling through Europe with my wife on our honeymoon, we arrived in Lucerne, Switzerland, late one night after being on the train for most of the day. We checked into a modest hotel, and outside the rain came down in a hard, noisy boil in the street. It was one of those cold-summer Alpine rains where drivers couldn't get it off their windshields fast enough to drive safely. And I had not yet run.

I stood in the lobby entrance for ten minutes and it became obvious that the weather wasn't likely to change any time soon. I brooded. I considered trudging back up to the room. The "sensible" excuses gathered like vultures on a branch, stacking up side by side. What's one day? Hell, it's my honeymoon!

Finally, I made a dash for this nearby famous landmark—an old covered bridge. I was drenched before I got there. Maybe the bridge was a hundred meters long, I can't remember. But for fifteen or twenty minutes, I trotted back and forth under cover of this bridge, the rain thundering on the roof—my shoes making a squishy sound with each step, like someone was squeezing a sponge. After a suitable interval, a pretense of dignity and dedication, I dashed back through the rain.

I am both proud of and embarrassed by that run. What kind of geek goes out and runs in a cloudburst just before midnight on his honeymoon? Me, I guess. But probably many others, too. You know who you are.

" "

"Believe in yourself, know yourself, deny yourself, and be humble."
> —**John Treacy**'s four principles of training prior to Los Angeles '84

◆

"The will to win means nothing without the will to prepare." —**Juma Ikangaa**, Tanzania

◆

"Somewhere in the world someone is training when you are not. When you race him, he will win."
> —**Tom Fleming**'s Boston Marathon training sign on his wall

◆

"One morning in Boston, it was snowing so hard that I didn't think anybody would be going training, but I went down to the track anyway. Billy [Smith] was there, though. He opened the door and said: 'The road to Mexico is out there.'"

—**David Hemery**, who won the 400-meter
hurdles at Mexico City in '68

◆

Someone once came up to **Duncan MacDonald** and said: "I saw you on television and read about you in the newspapers. How do you do it?" MacDonald answered: "I don't watch television and I don't read the papers."

◆

"It was *mano a mano*. The last great practitioner of that was George Young. He got up in the morning and thought: 'Goddamn it, those Russians have been training for hours.' He thought of that every morning. He is, as I am now, more objective about it."

—**Kenny Moore**, on training in the "old days"

◆

"I wish chiefly to impress on all athletes who may read this book that if they wish to excel at any branch of sport they must train. Train steadily, consistently, and constantly, and always bear in mind that however well they may be doing it is still possible for them to do better."
  —**Alf Shrubb**

◆

"You have to imagine that training is like a bow that you pull back as far as possible to shoot the arrow at an exact point in time. This can be dangerous. Sometimes you can't hold the bowstring back any longer. Or you can overpull it."
  —**Uta Pippig**

◆

"Live like a clock."
  —**Jumbo Elliott** of Villanova, on how runners should structure their lifestyle

◆

"I go by the axiom of training that Jumbo Elliott of Villanova used: KISS—Keep It Simple, Stupid."
  —**Marty Liquori**

◆

"A little kid comes riding up on his bike and asks: 'Gone a mile yet?' . . . I said 'Yeah, I've gone about five.' He says, 'Don't you hate running?'"
  —Don Kardong

◆

"I'd run from my house down two blocks and back and lie down on the ground and die."
  —Jim Ryun, on training himself at age fifteen

◆

"Running is a lot like life. Only ten percent of it is exciting. Ninety percent of it is slog and drudge."
  —Dave Bedford, English distance runner who occasionally put in 200 miles a week in training

◆

"A lot of people don't realize that about 98 percent of the running I put in is anything but glamorous: 2 percent joyful participation, 98 percent dedication! It's a tough formula. Getting out in the forest in the biting cold and the flattening heat, and putting in kilometer after kilometer."
  —Rob de Castella

◆

"This is a very tiresome job. Most of my time is devoted to thinking and running."

—**Juma Ikangaa**

◆

"I think there's only one sensible place for a person to be at 5:30 in the morning. That's in bed. And what am I doing? I'm out running. And I completely hate this."

—**Derek Clayton,** Australian marathoner, first to break 2:09

◆

"I was out training one black night when I heard a noise. I turned around and saw a leopard. I threw some stones at him and he went away, so I went on my way."

—**Filbert Bayi,** on training in Tanzania

◆

"If people saw you running in the street back then, they were likely to think you had stolen something."

—**Arturo Barrios** on training in Mexico City, 1978

◆

"All I know is that people don't throw beer cans at me when I run anymore."

—**John J. "Young John" Kelley,** 1995

"If one can stick to the training throughout the many long years, then will power is no longer a problem. It's raining? That doesn't matter. I am tired? That's besides the point. It's simply that I just have to."

—**Emil Zatopek**

◆

"We train every day of the year under all conditions. . . . A junior once asked me: 'What would we do if there was an earthquake and the epicenter was right here?' My answer was: 'Then we would run down the middle of the Earth!' "

—**Mario Moniz Pereira**, coach of Carlos Lopes

◆

"Stupid, blind determination forced me on, reeling along the streets until somehow I made the Halberg home. The rest were inside, dressed in track suits. I tottered in, collapsed on a sofa and burst into tears. It was most humiliating, but I just couldn't stop myself."

—**Peter Snell** on completing Lydiard's mountainous, 22-mile "soul-searching" Waiatarua run

◆

"In England, we don't shower as much as you do in America. It isn't really necessary. You're not really dirty, you know. I just sort of sponge off and dress. Besides, my A.M. workout isn't that fast."

—Ron Hill

"I still love to run, three to six miles a day. . . . But six or seven in the morning and ten more in the evening? No one loves to run that much. I don't mean running bores me. When you are among the best in the world at something, it doesn't bore you. . . . But you can never let your guard down. You can't go lie on the beach in the sun without worrying about the sun sapping you for the evening run. Everything you do is based on the two runs a day."

—Marty Liquori, training for the 1980 Olympics

"You have to go through cycles of extreme poverty and suffering for a while; they are used to that. . . . They get up early, run hard, rest, drink tea, get out and run hard again. When Simon Kirori gets up at 4 a.m.—I'm dedicated, but I'm not that dedicated."

—Keith Brantly, on why the Kenyan runners are so good, 1993

"No TV, no radio, no newspapers, not even a decent road; but I do not need any of them. Electric light we got here only last year."

—**Lasse Viren** on his training cabin in Lapland

"I think people can handle 150 to 200 miles a week. But something has to give somewhere. If he's a student, how's he going to study? He may be at the age of chasing and courtship, and that's an important form of sport and recreation, too."

—**Bill Bowerman**

"Man, that cat's late for work *every* morning."

—Conversation overheard by ultramarathoner **Ted Corbitt,** who used to run to the subway before work each day.

"For the working man, and more especially the married man, it is not easy to fit in around a hundred miles a week without conflict to social and family life. But with careful planning it can be done. . . . The best way to train twice a day is by running to work and back."

—**Ron Hill**

"In the '70s, I was a schoolteacher and trained at 5 a.m. and 5 P.M. During wintertime, I never saw the sun."
>   —**Tom Fleming**

◆

"With a marriage, you can change your mind."
>   —**Juma Ikangaa,** on the major difference between one's commitment to running and one's commitment to marriage

◆

"Running is my lover."
>   —**Toshihiko Seko,** when asked if he planned to marry

◆

"Some might say that it's easier to be the runner than the runner's family."
>   —**Rob de Castella**

◆

"Good things come slow—especially in distance running." —**Bill Dellinger,** Oregon coach

◆

"There was not a lot to do, and sitting around waiting for your red blood cells to multiply is not the most fascinating of pastimes."

   —**Brendan Foster** on summer altitude training at
    St. Moritz, Switzerland

◆

"In general, any form of exercise, if pursued continuously, will help to train us in perseverance. Long-distance running is particularly good training in perseverance."

   —**Mao Tse-Tung**, essay, 1918

◆

"The greatest treadmill running song, of course, is 'Black Dog' from Led Zeppelin IV."

   —**Pete Pfitzinger**, U.S. Olympic Marathoner

◆

"Training is principally an act of faith."

   —**Franz Stamfl**

◆

"There is nothing more monotonous and *sickening* than running round and round a track."

   —**Arthur Lydiard** on his aversion to pure
    interval training

"I don't think of running as 'training'. . . . 'Training' to me is repetition 220s and 440s, tough sessions on the road at near five-minute per mile pace, etc. If this is what the physiologists and sports specialist doctors have come up with to be a champ, then I must remain a mug runner and enjoy my evening sessions in the hills."
>   —**Jack Foster**

◆

"Training can get on a man's nerves. There is not use or profit in denying it."
>   —**Alf Shrubb**

◆

"All top international athletes wake up in the morning feeling tired and go to bed feeling very tired."
>   —**Brendan Foster**

◆

"Running is a big question mark that's there each and every day. It asks you, 'Are you going to be a wimp or are you going to be strong today?'"
>   —**Peter Maher,** Irish-Canadian Olympian and
>   sub-2:12 marathoner

◆

"Dead tired. Dog tired. Sore as hell. . . "
—Entries from **Laura Mykytok**'s training diary

◆

"Workouts are like brushing my teeth; I don't think about them, I just do them. The decision has already been made."
—**PattiSue Plumer**, U. S. Olympian

◆

"With Coach [Vin] Lananna, there's much improvisation during a workout. He'll always ask, 'How do you feel?' and if I'm looking good, then the workout gets harder."
—**Bob Kempainen,** U.S. Olympic marathoner

◆

"I just want to make sure it's living hell for anyone out there who's going to beat me."
—**Ken Souza,** champion duathlete on his hellish training regimen

◆

"There's a lot to be said for LSD—long, slow distance in this case."
—**Joe Henderson,** 1969

"Why should I practice running slow? I already know how to run slow. I want to learn to run fast. Everyone said: 'Emil, you are a fool!' But when I first won the European Championship, they said: 'Emil, you are a genius!'"

> —**Emil Zatopek**, concerning his emphasis on interval training

◆

"Long slow distance makes long slow runners."
> —**Jim Bush**, UCLA coach

◆

"I've never run more than seven miles in training—and that was six miles too long. I've always felt that long, slow distance produces long slow runners."
> —**Sebastian Coe**

◆

"Back at the quarry the heckling from the drivers and other workers increased and I responded with a defiant, 'Wait until I'm Olympic champion.' When I see them these days they acknowledge what the running madness led to."
> —**John Walker**, who, as a teenager, used to train on his lunch breaks from his 60-hours-a-week job at a quarry

"Most of the time we are running over hills and farms where there are a lot of gates and fences which help us to be good at the steeplechase. When I was living on my father's farm I used to run over obstacles all the time, chasing the cows and sheep."

—**Moses Kiptanui** on why the Kenyans are the
world's best steeplechasers

◆

"If I plan to enter this particular young man in a steeple-chase again, I owe it to his parents to make sure he knows how to fall without killing himself. I made him take swimming last year."

—**Bill Bowerman**, on why he made Kenny
Moore take gymnastics at Oregon

◆

"I have always been regarded as a mad trainer. The older, the madder."

—**Juha "the Cruel" Väätäinen**

◆

"I'll train like a madman, *un loco*. Well, not like a mad-man perhaps, but as if it were my last race."

—**Rudolfo Gomez**, prior to the Los Angeles
Olympic Games

"I've seen them training nowadays. If you'd seen me training with Cerutty you'd have been *frightened*."
—**Herb Elliott,** comment to Steve Ovett's coach

◆

"I don't want to plead that it's the life of a monk, but I can't think of a sport—with the possible exception of swimming—where people train as hard."
—**Sebastian Coe** on distance running

◆

"When you're running 190 miles a week, you do nothing else. You have to live like a monk."
—**Pablo Sierra,** 1994 Twin Cities Marathon winner, who trained three times a day for eight weeks

◆

"There is a great advantage in training under unfavorable conditions. It is better to train under bad conditions, for the difference is then a tremendous relief in a race."
—**Emil Zatopek**

◆

"I don't train. I just run my three to fifteen miles a day."
—**Jack Foster**

"The long run is what puts the tiger in the cat."
  —Bill Squires

◆

"Running was never anything natural to me. It took a long time for me to be able to run well, and I still don't look very good doing it. I had to do thirty- and thirty-five-mile runs in order to get my body attuned to running marathons, or I would just die off at twenty miles. Tenacity was my only gift."   **—Kenny Moore**

◆

"If you put down a good solid foundation and build one room after another, pretty soon you have a house. You build in your speedwork, your pace and increase your ability to run races and think races out. Then it's possible to run the way we do."
  —Rod Dixon

◆

"Everyone is an athlete. The only difference is that some of us are in training, and some are not."
  —Dr. George Sheehan

◆

"Basically, you have all these different types of training and different types of workouts. You've got general distance running, you've got fartlek, you've got hill work, you've got aerobic training sessions, you've got anaerobic training sessions and then you've got the rest phase. You take these phases and you arrange them in the right order."

—**Jerome Drayton**, winner of the 1977
Boston Marathon

◆

"The number of miles I have run since I was a toddler would have taken me around the world several times, and I still cannot define precisely my joy in running. There is no sacrifice in it. I lead what I regard a normal life. In my case, I thoroughly enjoy running a hundred-odd miles a week. If I didn't I wouldn't do it. Who can define happiness? To some, happiness is a warm puppy or a glass of cold beer. To me, happiness is running in the hills with my mates around me."

—**Ron Clarke**

◆

"My training was very one-sided. I practiced only in summer. Actual winter training was hardly known in those days. . . . I had no idea of speedwork, so it was no wonder I remained a slow trudger for so many years!"
   —Paavo Nurmi

◆

2. MODERATION IN THE TRAINING PROGRAM

"Train, don't strain."
   —Athletic proverb

◆

"Training is a case of stress management. Stress and rest, stress and rest."
   —Brooks Johnson

◆

Someone once reportedly asked **Jack Daniels**, coach of Div. III women's cross-country powerhouse Cortland State, about what kind of training was currently most popular among distance runners. Daniels simply responded: "Overtraining."

"In my dictionary, the word 'Overtrain' falls just a page away from the word 'Overkill', defined as 'to obliterate with more nuclear force than required.' Consider the connection: If your target is top running performance, then to overtrain means to apply more force than is required to hit that target. In fact, overtraining may literally obliterate your target, or at least leave you without the will to pursue it."

—Jack Daniels

◆

"Hard work will get you nowhere!"

> **—Jumbo Elliott,** advice to his runners the week of a big meet

◆

"Overtraining is the biggest problem incurred by runners who lack the experience or discipline to cope with their own enthusiasm."

—Marty Liquori

◆

"There are no magic workouts. It's about a willingness to cross boundaries."

> **—Peter Tegen,** coach at the University of Wisconsin

"I recall his [Dave Bedford's] training prior to the 1974 Commonwealth Games when he was injured. It was three sessions a day. In the morning he would go out and hammer himself. After a few hours rest he would train himself into the ground. The afternoon would be spent at the physio and then he would thrash himself at night."

—Rod Dixon

◆

"I wondered what would happen if I went beyond my 120-130 miles per week. Would I reach another plane of fitness and capability? I had to find out. . . But I was never really happy. A lot of the time I felt slightly fatigued and towards the end of this increased training stint I seemed to be doing nothing but changing in and out of running gear."

—Ron Hill

◆

"Long distance running is unnatural. I think the average person overdoes it. I don't think the body or the foot or anything was structured to run 100 miles a week."

—Dr. Richard Schuster, NYC podiatrist

◆

"Runners like to train 100 miles per week because it's a round number. But I think 88 is a lot rounder."
   —Don Kardong

◆

"If someone says, 'Hey, I ran 100 miles this week. How far did you run?' ignore him! What the hell difference does it make? . . . The magic is in the man, not the 100 miles." **—Bill Bowerman**

◆

"Well, well, well. Winning the Enschede [Marathon] at the end of a rest period, on an average of only 56 miles a week. And in 2:18:06, on a hot day, and with very little effort. It made me think. Yes! It made me think that 120 to 130 miles per week perhaps weren't absolutely necessary for good marathon performances."
   —Ron Hill, 1973

◆

"I leave my watch at home. Otherwise, it's a lost cause."
   —Todd Williams on what it takes for him to have
      an easy day

◆

"I don't wear a watch during my long runs. That way I am not tempted to compare my time from week to week."
   —Lynn Jennings

◆

"Everybody and his mother knows you shouldn't train hard on Friday if you have a race on Saturday. But Thursday is a little tricky; Thursday is the most dangerous day of the week."
   —Marty Stern

◆

"Rest on Sundays altogether. You will certainly feel strongly inclined for the lazyoff, and certainly will not suffer thereby."
   —Alf Shrubb

◆

"During the hard training phase never be afraid to take a day off. If your legs are feeling unduly stiff and sore, rest; if you are at all sluggish, rest; in fact, if in doubt, rest."
   —Bruce Fordyce

◆

"Just remember this: No one ever won the olive wreath with an impressive training diary."
   —Marty Liquori

"I find 140 miles per week is easy, but 160 is hard."
—**Tom Fleming,** 1979 while training for the
Boston Marathon

"We used to live in Coronado and there was this bike path with water on both sides—straight and boring. I used to hammer out a great two-hour run there, wind blowing, sun beating, no trees, no conversation, no other runners."
—**Thom Hunt,** world class runner in the 1980s

"You find out by trial and error what the optimal level of training is. If I found I was training too hard, I would drop it back for a day or two. I didn't run for five days before the sub-four-minute mile."
—**Sir Roger Bannister**

"Sex before the race? Fine, it will do you no harm. But try not to distract the starter."
—**Roger Robinson,** in *Heroes and Sparrows*

Fear

Bite on the bullet, old man, and don't let them think you're afraid.

—Rudyard Kipling

FEAR

Dick DeSchriver, my old college coach, remembers running a cross-country invitational race when he was an undergrad at Notre Dame. Wes Santee, the brash "Kansas Cowboy" and outstanding miler, was in the meet. Just prior to the gun, Santee allegedly loped out fifty yards, then turned—looked the field of rivals up and down—and announced in something more than a stage whisper: "Well, there's nobody here that can beat me!" Santee then went out and won the race. Well, as they say in Texas (or Kansas), "It ain't braggin' if you can do it."

But Santee was definitely a rare case. Even the great runners toe the line with a tad of apprehension, or run scared now and again. And the ones that don't look nervous might just be better actors. For example, a list of, say, the top dozen or so most gritty and gutsy competitors in the sport of long distance running would be incomplete if it did not include Gaston Roelants of Belgium. An Olympic gold medalist in the steeplechase at Tokyo in 1964, Roelants was a lion in any race, be it on the cross-country course (where he won three world titles), track, or roads. But even Roelants had to deal with fear of losing. French miler Michel Jazy is fond of telling this story:

Roelants once showed up for a twilight meet, entered in his strongest event—the 3000-meter steeplechase. But so, too, were a few of the better Scandinavian barrier specialists and Roelants—never known for blistering finishing speed—decided to start pushing the pace about the same time smoke emerged from the barrel of the starting pistol. If someone was going to beat Roelants, then that someone was going to pay in pain for seven and one-half laps—that was a given.

Around and around Roelants sped, clearing barriers and splashing in and out of the water hazard, forcing the pace. But someone was still there—he could tell by the shadow. So he ran faster. To the limit. Eight minutes and change, full of anxiety and self-inflicted torture. And, as he approached the last hurdle, *still* one of those damned Vikings was hovering just off his shoulder! How could that be? But, it was true, someone was still there, ruthlessly leeching off his hard work, poised to pounce in the homestretch and ready to steal the glory that rightfully belonged to the Belgian workhorse. So Roelants poured on more steam, over the last barrier, sprinting to the finish with all he could muster.

Then it was over. Roelants had held on—only to discover that the Scandinavians were way back. It was simply that the lights around the track had reflected in such a manner that his *own* shadow appeared to be that of a competitor's. In essence, the great Roelants, as tough a man as anyone who ever laced on racing shoes, had been scared of his own shadow.

" "

Longtime Atoms TC coach **Fred Thompson** told Vic Ziegel of the New York Daily News how six-year-olds often react when they line up for their first competition in the New York's Colgate Games: "They stand on the line and pee on themselves. We always keep a mop near the start."

◆

"Fear is a great motivator."
— **John Treacy**, 1984 Olympic Marathon silver medalist

"The good ones pretend they don't train hard, the bad ones say they train like Olympic champions. They're never completely fit and never completely well. If an athlete ever admits to being ready for competition, without the slightest injury, raring to go and sure to win, you know it's time to send for the jacket with the laces up the back." —**Pat Butcher**, British journalist

◆

"When the meal was over we all had a quiet rest in our rooms and I meditated on the race. This is the time when an athlete feels all alone in the big world. Opponents assume tremendous stature. Any runner who denies having fears, nerves or some kind of disposition is a bad athlete, or a liar."
—Gordon Pirie

◆

"I have never been a killer. I'm not an aggressive personality and if I can remember any emotion I felt during a race it was fear. The greatest stimulator of my running was fear."
—Herb Elliott

◆

"I limbered up just a little before entering the stadium, and even so I felt a twinge in my thigh, no doubt the fruit of my imagination. And I went back to the massage room so that my faithful Morizot could take the trouble off my muscles. This soothed me considerably and I thought I was back to a normal state until somebody summoned me to the starting line. It was like feeling a blade go through my flesh."

—**Jules Ladoumegue**, French miler of the 1930s, on pre-race nerves

◆

"As I stepped onto the track I felt my legs go rubbery. I saw over a 100,000 people in the stands, and before I knew it, I had collapsed onto the infield grass. 'Can it be,' I remembered thinking, as I lay there gazing up at the sky, 'that I'm so nervous I'm not going to be able to run?' Then I realized how ridiculous I'd look, flat on my back on the grass as they started the race. I guess the humor of that image made me lose my nervousness. I was able to recover, get up and jog to the starting line."

—**Tom Courtney**, on the moments before he won the Olympic 800 gold in Melbourne

◆

"The new Kenyans. There are always new Kenyans."
   —**Noureddine Morcelli**, 1988, when asked if he
      feared any other runners

◆

"I prefer to remain in blissful ignorance of the opposition.
That way I'm not frightened by anyone's reputation."
   —**Ian Thompson**, who ran a 2:09:12 marathon
      at the 1974 Commonwealth Games

◆

"Everyone was frightened of Grete. If Grete would have
gone to the restroom on the course, Julie Brown would
have followed her."
   —**Johan Kaggestand**, Grete Waitz's coach, on her
      World Marathon Championship win in 1983

◆

"Jogging through the forest is pleasant, as is relaxing by
the fire with a glass of gentle Bordeaux and discussing
one's travels. Racing is another matter. The front-
runner's mind is filled with an anguished fearfulness, a
panic, which drives into pain."
   —**Kenny Moore**

◆

"No one knows the fear in a front runner's mind more than me. When you set off at a cracking pace for four or five laps and find that your main rivals are still breathing down your neck, that's when you start to panic."
   —Ron Clarke

◆

"The thing that makes [Bob] Kennedy so good is that he doesn't have a fear of losing. He was willing to go to Europe and get hammered."
   —Frank Shorter

◆

"He cleared the hurdles like he feared they had spikes imbedded on the top, and leaped the water hazard as if he thought crocodiles were swimming in it."
   —A description of Kenya's Amos Biwotts' 8:51.0 steeplechase win in Mexico City

◆

"Big occasions and races which have been eagerly anticipated almost to the point of dread, are where great deeds can be accomplished."
   —Jack Lovelock

◆

"Fear is the strongest driving-force in competition. Not fear of one's opponent, but of the skill and high standard which he represents; fear, too, of not acquitting oneself well. In the achievement of greater performances, of beating formidable rivals, the athlete defeats fear and conquers himself."

—**Franz Stampfl,** *Stampfl on Running*

◆

"I say I'm going to finish last. That takes the pressure off. I'm in such a nervous frenzy at the starting line, I'm shaking."

—**Dan Middleman,** 1996 U.S. Olympian
in the 10,000-meter run

◆

"The Games have hardly begun and already I wish they would end because I am so scared."

—**Marie-Jose Perec,** France's "Gazelle" and
two-time defending Olympic champ in
the 400 meters. She fled Sydney in 2000
before her event.

Racing

Every morning in Africa, a gazelle wakes up. It knows it must outrun the fastest lion or it will be killed. Every morning in Africa, a lion wakes up. It knows it must run faster than the slowest gazelle, or it will starve. It doesn't matter whether you're a lion or a gazelle—when the sun comes up, you'd better be running.

  —**Inspirational sign** on a runner's office wall

RACING

I propose that there are two kinds of runners. One is the runner as animal—competitor, predator, survivalist. This theory says the successful runner toughens himself with self-sacrifice and Spartan-like preparation. There is talk of being *worthy*; of giving up the finer things in life—wine, women, and, perhaps, even song. These are runners who traditionally go off and train from a cabin in the remote forest; gasp around at 10,000 feet in oxygen-thin air; dash up and down sweeping sand dunes in bare feet.

The other type is the runner as artist. The late Steve Prefontaine (arguably both animal and artist) once said: "A race is like a work of art." The ultimate runner/artist—at least when his or her powers are at their zenith—is not satisfied with just winning. Instead, *how* the race is won is important—as Salazar (in "The Marathon" chapter, page 177) explains, the great bull-fighters were not content to merely kill the bull; they risked death to fight *El Toro* in an honorable fashion. Uta Pippig talks about presenting the "beauty of the marathon."

Just as the runner/animal tempers both body and soul

in the roaring forge of daily training, so does the runner/artist spend time in preparation. The runner/animal bristles for the battle; the runner/artist prepares for the unveiling of the masterpiece.

Of course, it takes a certain kind of bravery to race. It takes incredible willpower to "train like an animal" for months and years—with no guarantees, figuratively speaking, of a payoff. It takes courage to present your race—if only to yourself—as an artist presents a painting. In a sense, when you prepare for a big race, you say: "Okay, this is what I've been working on for the last four months."

How fast, or where you finish, doesn't necessarily count for everything. But how you raced against yourself counts for almost all. Inevitably, most runners eventually conclude that the race is against themselves—and how you conduct yourself in the face adversity, or how you bounce back from defeat, can often mean more than a time or place.

John Landy is famous as the guy who glanced over his left shoulder to see where Roger Bannister was in the "Mile of the Century" race in Vancouver—as Bannister whipped by on his right. But Landy once ran a mile race in Australia where he inadvertently tripped a young runner. Landy stopped, yanked the young man back to his feet, and resumed running. Landy won the race, and gained the nickname "Gentleman John." The young man, whose name was Ron Clarke, moved up to longer distances and set several world records.

Now, the runner-as-animal theorists would probably subscribe to a "do what's necessary to win" philosophy. Landy's benevolent instincts leaned more toward the runner-as-artist. I would submit that this particular race was one of Landy's masterpieces. Certainly, he wanted to win (and did)—but he did so with deference to his fellow runner and to his ingrained sense of fair play. He would have made a great bullfighter.

" "

"Yet that man is happy and poets sing of him who conquers with hand and swift foot and strength."
—**Pindar**, Greek poet, 500 B.C.

◆

"First is first, and second is nowhere."
>   —**Ian Stewart**, British 1500/5000 star

◆

"Second place is not a defeat. It is a stimulation to get better. It makes you even more determined."
>   —**Carlos Lopes**, Portugal, prior to 1984 Games

◆

"Racing teaches us to challenge ourselves. It teaches us to push beyond where we thought we could go. It helps us to find out what we are made of. This is what we do. This is what it's all about."
>   —**PattiSue Plumer**, U.S. Olympian

◆

"That is the sort of race which one really enjoys—to feel at one's peak on the day when it is necessary, and to be able to produce the pace at the very finish. It gives a thrill which compensates for months of training and toiling. But it is the sort of race that one wants only about once a season."
>   —**Jack Lovelock**, diary entry on beating
>   Bonthron in WR time of 4:07.6. Bonthron
>   also broke the old mark

"Everyone in life is looking for a certain rush. Racing is where I get mine."
  —John Trautmann

◆

"If you want to win a race you have to go a little berserk."
  —Bill Rodgers

◆

"I tell our runners to divide the race into thirds. Run the first part with your head, the middle part with your personality, and the last part with your heart."
  —Mike Fanelli, club coach

◆

"Those who say that I will lose and am finished will have to run over my body to beat me."
  —Said Aouita

◆

"Remember to 'bank' your racing powers until you seriously require them, and you will then find that the interest is there as well as the capital when you start to draw on the account."
  —Arthur Newton

◆

"The race is not always to the swift, but to those who keep on running."

—Nike running poster

◆

"A runner's creed: I will win; if I cannot win, I shall be second; if I cannot be second, I shall be third; if I cannot place at all, I shall still do my best."

—Ken Doherty

◆

"People are yelling at me, 'You're the best! You're the best!' and I'm goin', 'Hey, guys, I'm almost walking.'"

—Mark Allen, description of trying to catch the leader in the 1993 Ironman triathlon

◆

"I haven't seen too many American distance men on the international scene willing to take risks. I saw some U.S. women in Barcelona willing to risk, more than men. The Kenyans risk. Steve Prefontaine risked. I risked—I went through the first half of the Tokyo race just a second off my best 5000 time."

—Billy Mills

◆

"My whole feeling in terms of racing is that you have to be very bold. You sometimes have to be aggressive and gamble."

—Bill Rodgers

◆

"At this point (the backstretch), I abandoned the studied relaxation. This is the moment when you stop consciously controlling what you are doing and pour everything into driving out the utmost speed."

—Peter Snell

◆

"Coming off the last turn, my thoughts changed from 'One more try, one more try, one more try. . .' to 'I can win! I can win! I can win!'"

—Billy Mills

◆

"Don't quit, dammit!"

—Marty Liquori to Kip Keino during their 1972 race at Villanova when Keino backed off on the gun lap

◆

"At the bell, I gave just one quick glance behind me and took in the situation in all its ghastliness. The wall at my heels was thick. . . . I had put in a couple of sixty second laps and almost everybody was still chasing me, damn it! I was the fugitive now, and I realized I had to flee as if my life depended on it. . . . In the far turn I had the most frightening experience of my career. Some guy in black was forcing himself by me. It was Quax [of New Zealand], whom I really hadn't reckoned very seriously . . . . I found my last gear and it was just enough. The black shadow glided away from my eyes. The holy sanctuary of the finish line engulfed me—I had won!"

    —**Lasse Viren** on his 5000 victory in Montreal

◆

"If we can't beat this guy on his honeymoon, we never will."

    —**Cary Weisiger,** on Peter Snell's California
       tour in '63

◆

"Road racing is rock 'n roll; track is Carnegie Hall."
    —**Marty Liquori**

◆

"When you experience the run, you regress back to the mandrill on the savannah eluding the enclosing pride of lions that is planning to take your very existence away. Not only that, but you relive the hunt. Running is about 30 miles of chasing prey that can outrun you in a sprint, and tracking it down and bringing life back to your village. It's a beautiful thing."
—Shawn Found

◆

2. RACING TACTICS

"Never really give in as long as you have any earthly chance, and above all don't allow yourself to fancy that you are in this predicament until the gruesome knowledge is absolutely forced upon you. For however bad you may be feeling, it is by no means impossible that the other fellows may be feeling quite as much, if not even more, distressed."
—Alf Shrubb

◆

"The only tactics I admire are do-or-die."

  —Herb Elliott

◆

"There's only one way to beat Elliott. That's to tie his legs together."

  —Ron Delany, after running 3:57.5 to Elliott's
  3:54.5 world record in Dublin

◆

"If you have got in front you will, as already advised, use your utmost endeavors to keep there. It's the best place to be, you know."

  —Alf Shrubb

◆

"Never take the lead unless you really want it, and if you take it, do something with it. . . Once in the lead, you have only two options, either you are going to pick up the pace, or you are going to slow it down. Once in control, a fast pace usually insures the fastest runner will win, a slow pace perhaps the fastest runner will still win but occasionally the race will go to the best kicker."

  —Tom Courtney, 1956 Olympic 800 champ

◆

"After 5 or 6 laps I have read everyone like a newspaper. and I know who is able to do this or that. And I know what I am able to do."

—Miruts Yifter

◆

"The problem with big kickers is they often lose to *other* big kickers."

—Harry Groves, Penn State coach

◆

"Don't struggle and burst yourself every yard. There is no sense in making a quarter-mile race of a section of the course between yourself and your immediate attendants, so as to crack you all up and leave the field open for the others to jog comfortably in."

—Alf Shrubb

◆

"The idea that you can't lose contact with the leaders has cut more throats than it has saved."

—Arthur Lydiard

◆

"Even [Glenn] Cunningham, strong though he is, could not live up to the strain of setting such a pace, combined with the mental worry of having a lightly-stepping black shadow right on his shoulder, locking strides with him, almost breathing in his ear—for the trick of shadowing an opponent within sight and hearing is one of the more maddening and distracting forms of tactics that one can use in any race."

—**Jack Lovelock,** diary entry

◆

"I would never use Rod [Dixon] as a pace man. Off the track, we are good friends, but on the track we are very competitive. It's me for me and Rod for Rod, right, mate?"

—**John Walker**

◆

"Eleven stupid men."

—**An observer's comment** when the Barcelona Olympic 1500 started out at a very slow pace. Twelve runners comprised the final.

◆

"I guess I prefer to stay unpredictable so that people cannot say, 'Dixon's a front-runner' or 'Dixon, he stays back in the pack and then comes up strong at the end.' Strategy, my dear. I don't mind setting the pace, though, when I have to run my own race. I do what the situation requires."

—Rod Dixon

◆

"Perhaps the most intriguing, yet at the same time most tragic aspect of distance running is racing strategies and tactics or the lack of them. A slight hesitance, a single step to the inside, a few seconds miscalculation of the right pace of the timing of the final kick, and any other seemingly minor error, may throw away months and years of careful preparation and sacrifice. The race is not always to either the swift or the strong, but to the clever, the skillful, and the constantly wary."

—Ken Doherty

◆

"The days of tactics are numbered."

—Arthur Lydiard

◆

Records

If you want to get somewhere else, you must run at least twice as fast as that.

—**Lewis Carroll,** *Through the Looking Glass*

RECORDS

On tour in the United States in the 1940s, Swedish miler Gunder Hägg was awakened early one morning in New York City. Before he was even given an explanation, Hägg instinctively blurted out: "Which of my records has been broken?" In fact, that was precisely what had happened— his friendly rival Arne Andersson had broken Hägg's world 1500m record back in Sweden. Hägg quickly packed his bags, saying: "I better go home before he breaks the rest of my records."

World records are precious. For most of history's great runners, the desirability of a world record is surpassed only by that for an Olympic medal. The allure, however, of world records in track and field is that the performer, in essence, exists (if only ever so fleetingly) where no runner before them has ever been.

But rarely in this day and age does someone suggest that a record that's just been set is in any way "unbeatable." It's generally assumed that someone, somewhere, will eventually run that several tenths of a second faster in the 800 or mile; ten seconds faster in the 10,000; whatever it takes. Still, it gets a little tricky when you consider the bottom-line absolute—that is, *no one will ever run a race in nothing flat.*

Therefore, there is a limit to how fast, say, an 800-meter race can be run. Sebastian Coe's world record of 1:41.73 endured for sixteen years, until Wilson Kipketer first tied, then bettered the Englishman's mark in the summer of 1997. Kipketer was well aware the track journalists would crave more: "I am very satisfied for now. . . . Please don't ask me about breaking 1:40!" he implored the scribblers.

Similarly, Jim Ryun's high school mile record stood for so long that more than a few fans assumed it was far beyond the reach of any kid from the MTV, WorldWideWeb generation. At least until Alan Webb—a.k.a. The Webbmaster— erased Ryun's record (3:55.3 set in 1965!) at the 2001 Prefontaine Classic with his jaw-dropping 3:53.43. But can the next Alan Webb—somewhere in America—be lacing on his training shoes right now? Or will Webb's record, like Ryun's, last for three and a half decades?

English miler Steve Cram suggested that records in the future will rarely be the result of training breakthroughs or technical advances (better tracks or racing shoes), but from the odd "freak" who simply is blessed with great physical and psychological tools, and who is just slightly better than those that came before. It seems correct to say that all records are "breakable"—but one day we will have to be wrong. When?

"Bid me run, and I will strive with things impossible."
—**Shakespeare,** *Julius Caesar*

◆

"It is like a dream come true, I tell the journalists after the race. One of them later writes that this seems too hackneyed to describe such an emotional occasion. Well, what does he expect after a world record? Shakespeare?"
—**Brendan Foster,** after setting world 3000
record at Gateshead, England

◆

"Records are made to be broken."
—**Athletic proverb**

◆

"Dream barriers look very high until someone climbs them. Then they are not barriers anymore."
—**Lasse Viren**

◆

"Dimly I could hear the crowd chanting 'Walker, Walker, Walker' as the people of Göteborg supported a man from a country they hardly knew existed except for the athletes in black."
—**John Walker,** en route to his 3:49.4 world mile
record in Sweden

"Time is the enemy. Time is what we are fighting in our lives, as we fight it in our running. We can never achieve a total victory, but every time we achieve a partial one, every time we extend the boundaries of man's capacity, we affirm our human dignity. In the air, we have flown faster than sound. On the ground, we have broken the barrier of the four-minute mile. In the operating theater and laboratory, we have learned ways to prolong the life of the human body far beyond what was ever dreamed. The day will come when each human being will be able to choose for himself exactly how long he wants to live, just as the day will come when we travel not merely beyond the speed of sound, but beyond the speed of light. Every record that is broken on the running track, on water, in the air, on the salt flats, is a gesture of human independence. The day will come when we will smash every clock in the world, because we shall have conquered time, and clocks will no longer be necessary."

—Coach **Sam Dee** in *The Olympian*

◆

"I'm afraid that record attempts are not in my line and this has strengthened my opposition to such a race."

—**Jack Lovelock**, diary entry after missing a
world record attempt at 1500 meters

"After I did it the bloody place was in an uproar. There were people coming over the fence and on to the track. The noise level was deafening. However, the real fun started when I tried to leave the arena. Everybody wanted to touch me for luck and there were 20,000 people there! It was a real Irish thing. Journalist Harry Gordon and some other people surrounded me like a wedge to get me off the track and under the stand. The dressing rooms were in a great big tin shed out the back. Harry Gordon ran around saying he'd had all the buttons ripped off his coat trying to push people away. All I could hear continually was: 'Let me touch you for luck lad.' I was taken out through the back of the shed between two sheets of tin and finally escaped through a hole in the fence out to the bus. I think it was the first world record ever broken in Ireland and the crowd was very excited."

—**Albie Thomas**, Aussie distance ace, on
breaking the world 3 mile record at Dublin's
Santry track in 1958

◆

"Dixon and Agnew raced to me, hugging me. Agnew thrust a stopwatch so close under my nose I could not read it. He seemed to be demented, shouting over and over. 'What?' I yelled. 'You're under 3:50! You're under 3:50!' he screamed. I thought for an awful moment that he and Dixon might try and kiss me."

—John Walker

◆

"People wanted me to go everywhere to run. When I was running in Finland, there would be a meet promoter from Italy. When I was running in Italy, there would be one from Japan, and Australia and New Zealand. All over you know? I know that I became very confused; it is such a new experience and you are not sure why people are so crazy about you. There was all the travel and changes in time and people pushing me to do things I didn't want to do. People wanted me to go there and there and there and there. It was like they didn't even think I was a human being like them; I was an extraordinary person to them, a machine they thought could do anything."

—Henry Rono on setting four world
records in 1978

"I'm not a machine that can be wound up every day."
>—**Herb Elliott**, following his WR 1500 in
> Göteborg, Sweden, and being asked to run
> sub-4 the next night in Malmo

"It's a shame for track and field. When I was the world record holder, I ran against everyone. But now, people are scared of their reputations."
>—**John Walker**, July 1981

"It becomes luggage permanently attached to your name. It matters not what else you do. You'll be introduced everywhere as world-record holder in the mile. Even after you're hurt or on the downside of your career, you'll believe you can do anything. It can create great frustration."
>—**Steve Cram**

"It's a strange feeling to break a world record and still lose."
>—**Glenn Cunningham**, after his 3:48.0 1500,
> losing to Princeton's Bill Bonthron by
> one-tenth of a second

"Losing five or six seconds in the fall is a good indication that my record can be considerably improved. In my opinion, twenty-seven minutes will be broken one day—not by me, but I am sure that I will live long enough to see it broken."
       —Lasse Viren

◆

"I suffered the woes of hell down the homestretch, yet I think I would have tortured myself to go a bit faster if I had known I was that close to the European record."
       —Michel Jazy, France, 3:38.4, 2nd to Elliott's
       3:35.6 in Rome Olympics

◆

"To boast of a performance which I cannot beat is merely stupid vanity. And if I can beat it that means there is nothing special about it. What has passed is already finished with. What I find more interesting is what is still to come." **—Emil Zatopek**

◆

"There can be, to me, no ultimate at the present time, for I am unable to see where, as our knowledge of physiology and psychology increases, there can be any limits to the human capacity for speed."
       —Jack Lovelock, diary entry, 1930s

"All Stockholm knew that Lovelock's record was trembling."
  —**Sportswriter** prior to Hägg breaking the
    1500 meter mark in 1941.

"It is a paradox to say the human body has no 'limit.' There must be a limit to the speed at which men can run. I feel this may be around 3:30 for the mile. However, another paradox remains—if an athlete manages to run 3:30, another runner could be found to marginally improve on that time."
  —**Sir Roger Bannister**

"It's a psychological as well as physical barrier; the woman who breaks it [the 2:20 marathon] will undoubtedly usher in a new age in the sport of running, the way Roger Bannister did when he shattered the four-minute mile." —**Joan Benoit Samuelson**

"It's important to be the first to run under 2:20. It's a barrier and if I do it, then others will see they can too. My record is 2:21:06 and I feel it is very possible to run one minute faster. I feel 2:18 is possible within 4 or 5 years." —**Ingrid Kristiansen**, 1986

"Now I want to find out, How fast can I go? Can I run under 2:20 for a marathon? Okay, if I don't do it, it's not a catastrophe, but the question still hasn't been answered. I want to take a fair shot at making an answer."

    —Uta Pippig, 1994

◆

"The two-hour Marathon. The thing that can't be done. The mark they talk about in whispers."

        —Bill Persons, fictional coach in Hugh
            Atkinson's *The Games*

◆

"I think the idea of a two-hour marathon is thoroughly ridiculous. Absolutely ridiculous. I cannot foresee, *ever*, anyone breaking two hours."

        —Derek Clayton

◆

"By the year 2000, I predict that men will break the two-hour marathon."

        —Fred Lebow, 1984

◆

"It has not quite gone—but that's athletics."

        —Sebastian Coe, after Wilson Kipketer tied his
            longstanding 800m WR of 1:41.73 in July 1997

"If you trained hard perhaps you could beat me. I am only a human being, not a machine."

> —**Haile Gebrselassie,** WR holder in the 5000 (12:39.36) and 10,000 (26:22.75)

◆

"Records are intended to be broken. This [Ryun's own U.S. high school mile record] was such a barrier, it impeded the progress of high school miling."

> —**Jim Ryun**

◆

"I wanted that record today. . . . This means everything to me, to run on the track where Steve Prefontaine, one of my childhood heroes, ran."

> —**Alan Webb,** on breaking the U.S. high school mile record with 3:53.43

◆

"He [Webb] has the face of a big champion. You can see the fighting spirit in his face."

> —**Hicham El Gerrouj,** mile WR holder, after winning the 2001 Prefontaine Classic Mile, in which Alan Webb placed fifth, setting his high school mile record.

Cross-Country

These high wild hills
and rough uneven ways
draw out our miles
and make them wearisome.
—**Shakespeare,** *Richard II*

CROSS-COUNTRY

Watching a big cross-country meet from a distance is kind of like observing the Charge of the Light Brigade. There's this fascination with the pageantry, the ritual, the colors, the hundreds of runners who eventually combine to form a long, winding snake that flows through the course. And there is the course itself—grassy fields, trees bursting in autumnal splendor. And, perhaps, an ever-present feeling of respect (and envy) that the participants are meeting a lofty challenge.

It's not war, of course—but in the athletic sense, people are fighting for their honor out there. Runners and coaches talk about "attacking" or "dying" on the big hills, they talk of sacrifice and endurance, tactics and strategy. ("Always mystify, mislead, and surprise," said Civil War general Thomas "Stonewall" Jackson.)

Then again, if you're actually racing you can't appreciate the scenery too much, unless you took it all in during the warmup. You check out the highlights and make some mental notes: the steepest hill, the boggy spot along the creek, the hair-pin curve (where you and 300 other runners all think, "Hey, now here's a good place to make a move . . ."), the tree that marks one mile to go.

In the mega-races, in fact, it's quite possible to see nothing but some other runner's back from almost the very start—until you fling yourself across the finish line, stumble through the chute and—yes, collapse on somebody's sweat-drenched singlet in front of you. Inevitably, there's some official bellowing: "Come on! Run through the chute! Keep it movin'. . . Keep it movin'!" But you're bent over, gasping, admiring with salt-stung eyes the good, honest mud of battle, the trickle of blood from a spike wound, splattered on your still-quivering legs and too-old (but still lucky) racing shoes. What could be more beautiful?

One of my favorite snippets on *real* cross-country running is from *Drums Along The Mohawk*, a historical novel by Walter D. Edmonds. The story is set during the American Revolution in New York State's Mohawk Valley—and one chapter is titled: "Adam Helmer's Run." (There was a real life Adam Helmer who did make an actual run quite like that described by the author.)

Helmer, a frontier scout, is running to warn the settlers at German Flats of an impending attack (directed by

British agents) from Mohawk Indians. Trailed by a pack of running warriors, the scout has plenty of motivation to run fast. The Indians have been trying to run him down (over a woodland trail and across brooks) with "surge" tactics—one man sprinting up at a time, while the other warriors pace themselves until it's their turn.

> As he chanced a backward glance, he saw that the Indians were going to try and run him down now. The new man was there and it was evident that he was their best man. . .
>
> The Indian's legs moved with great rapidity. He had already taken his tomahawk from his belt as if he were confident of being able to haul up on the white man. The gesture gave Adam the incentive he needed. He was enraged, and he took his rage out in his running. . .
>
> It was the greatest running the Indian had ever looked at. He knew he was licked, and he started slowing up very gradually. By the time Adam hit the woods, the Indian had stopped and sat down by the roadside.
>
> When Adam looked back from the woods, the Indian wasn't even looking at him. He was all alone in the clearing and he was futilely

banging the ground between his legs with his tomahawk. Adam knew he had made it. He did not stop, nor even let down quickly on his pace. All he had to race now was time. He would have laughed if he could have got the breath for it. Time? Time, hell!

Which goes to show that there are, in fact, some cross-country races that you just cannot afford to lose.

"   "

"All I knew was that you had to run, run, run, without knowing why you were running . . . through fields that you didn't understand, and woods that made you afraid, over hills without knowing you'd been up and down."
   —**Colin Smith**, in Alan Sillitoe's *The Loneliness of the Long-Distance Runner*

◆

"Stadiums are for spectators. We runners have nature and that is much better." —**Juha Väätäinen**, Finland

"In the 4000-meter cross country race Mike Murphy the trainer gave me some hop before the start. I fainted after finishing the race and was out for several hours. Once I came to but could not move or open my eyes and felt them give me a shot of more hop. I feared it would be an overdose and kill me. Then I heard papa say in a calm voice: 'Will the boy live?' and Murphy reply 'I think he will, but can't tell.'"

> —**George S. Patton Jr.**, remembering his
> Stockholm Olympic cross-country race, the
> fifth and final event of the Military Pentathlon.
> He placed 3rd in the run, 5th overall out of 43
> Pentathlon entrants.

◆

"At the end of the cross-country run he fell insensible after crossing the line, but sustained no serious injury."

> —**Lt. Col. Frederick S. Foltz**, reporting on Patton
> to his superiors

◆

"The start of a World Cross Country event is like riding a horse in the middle of a buffalo stampede. It's a thrill if you keep up but one slip and you're nothing but hoof prints."—**Ed Eyestone**

"And if any of you want some tips on running, don't be in a hurry, and never let any of the other runners know you are in a hurry even if you are. You can always overtake on long-distance running without letting others smell the hurry in you."

> —**Colin Smith,** in *The Loneliness of the Long-Distance Runner*

◆

"The freedom of cross-country is so primitive. It's woman versus nature."

> —**Lynn Jennings**

◆

"Cross-country is like poker. You have to be holding five good cards all the time."

> —**Rollie Geiger,** North Carolina State coach

◆

"The footing was really atrocious. I loved it. I really like cross-country; you're one with the mud." Daniel!

> —**Lynn Jennings,** after winning the 1984 cross-country nationals

◆

"I prefer running without shoes. My toes didn't get cold. Besides, if I'm in front from the start, no one can step on them." —**Michelle Dekkers,** the barefoot South African runner who won the 1989 NCAA cross-country title for Indiana

"Get out well, but not too quickly, move through the field, be comfortable. Strategy-wise, go with your strengths. If you don't have a great finish, you must get away to win. I've always found it effective to make a move just before the crest of a hill. You get away just a little and you're gone before your opponent gets over the top. Also, around a tight bend, take off like holy hell. I've done that a number of times. . . . You should not be flying down the home straight. Most of your efforts should have been put forth earlier."
—**John Treacy,** Ireland's two-time world cross-country champion (1978, 1979)

"We told our guys to hold on for thirty minutes of agony for twelve months of glory."
—**Coach John McDonnell,** after Arkansas won the 1993 NCAA Cross-Country title

"When I was about fourteen or fifteen, and running in a pretty muddy cross-country race, one of my shoes stuck in the mud and came off. Boy, was I wild. To think that I had trained hard for this race and didn't do up my shoelace tightly enough! I really got aggressive with myself, and I found myself starting to pass a lot of runners. As it turned out, I improved something like twenty places in that one race. . . . But I never did get my shoe back!"
　　—Rob de Castella

◆

School cross-country runs started because the rugby pitches were flooded. There was an alternative—extra studying. This meant there were plenty of runners on sports afternoons."
　　—Gordon Pirie

◆

"Plasticized cross-country."
　　—Mike Manley, on the steeplechase

◆

"A running machine that glides over mud, crud and goop."
　　　　—Ed Eyestone's definition of Kenyan ace John
　　　　Ngugi (Goo Gee)

"The secret of cross country is to do everything we do on the track and take it into the bush."

—**Mike Koskei**, former national coach of Kenya

◆

"Is it really true that a seven-mile cross-country run is enforced upon all in this division, from generals to privates? . . . It looks to me rather excessive. A colonel or a general ought not to exhaust himself in trying to compete with young boys across country seven miles at a time. The duty of officers is no doubt to keep themselves fit, but still more to think of their men, and to take decisions affecting their safety and comfort. Who is the general of this division, and does he run the seven miles himself? If so, he may be more useful for football than for war. Could Napoleon have run seven miles across country at Austerlitz? Perhaps it was the other fellow he made run. In my experience, based on many years' observation, officers with high athletic qualifications are not usually successful in the higher ranks."

—**Sir Winston Churchill**, 1941, note for the
　　Secretary of State for War

Hills

The struggle itself toward the heights is enough to fill man's heart. One must imagine Sisyphus happy.

—**Albert Camus,** *The Myth of Sisyphus*

HILLS

Don Kardong once did an article on marathon advice—a nuts and bolts beginner's guide that covered everything from pre-race meals to proper pacing. Under the topic of hills, however, Kardong simply wrote:

"Hills: You entered a marathon with hills? You idiot."

Some runners *like* hills. I am one. In fact, I wish track races had hills in them, preferably just uphills. It might even things out a bit with those guys who got in line twice when God was handing out fast-twitch muscle fiber.

But I do agree with Kardong; nobody should have to run twenty-six miles *and* lots of hills, too; at least not with a stopwatch ticking. And in marathons you already have the heat factor; so why add hills to create a potentially lethal mix? (Did somebody just say: "Atlanta"?)

Cross-country is different. Cross-country, by definition, should have a few rollers, preferably with mud at the bottom. People who like flat cross-country courses should be playing lawn tennis or snooker-pool.

Spectators, of course, like hills, especially at marathons. Hills increase the chances for disaster. The same kind of gleefully sadistic running fans who gather around the water hazard during a steeplechase are likely to seek out a significant hill on a marathon course. Try to find a front row spot around Heartbreak Hill on Patriot's Day. You've got a better chance of getting a ticket to Boston Garden with the Celtics in the finals. Some people *enjoy* watching runners scrape their chins on their shoelaces.

Of course, runners who really love hills don't bother with hills at all—they run mountains. Stuff like the Pike's Peak Marathon and the Mt. Washington Road Race. The old joke here is: "It's easy. . . . Just one hill!" And if it's more than one hill you're interested in, well, check out some ultras such as the Western States 100 or the South Africa's Comrades Marathon, where you can do a good 10K—in vertical elevation changes.

Speaking for myself, a hellish uphill is better than a plunging descent. In fact, I'd say my scariest racing experience occurred during the Tour of Tameside, a multi-stage race (six races in seven days) held in England. The second day at Tameside involved a six-mile "fell" run, fells being a quaint term for nasty, rocky little mountains. Ron Hill, the race founder, broke his wrist coming down it one year—a little tidbit of information he felt compelled to share with me the night before I was going to run it.

After several miles of uphill, the course dropped abruptly over the "lip" and down, down, down a wispy, serpentine path (virtually impossible to stay on) through a boulder field, to the finish. Race volunteers with outstretched arms and eyes wide with alert tried to catch any would-be Humpty Dumpties.

With a little luck and some heartfelt pleas to the supreme creator, I did arrive at the bottom in one piece. My quads, however, had endured a heavy pounding. As I stood in line for a post-race massage, muttering "Never again, never again. . ." to myself, an older veteran tapped me on the shoulder. I would guess that he was a Scotsman, except I was able to understand him.

"Don't ye have fell roonin' in the States, lad?" he asked.

"Oh, yeah, we have it," I said. "But we call it hang-gliding and we usually issue helmets before we try it."

" "

"The introduction of resistance in form of sand and hill is too important to be ignored."
   —**Percy Cerutty**

◆

"Hills are speedwork in disguise."
   —**Frank Shorter**

◆

"Hills are the only beneficial type of resistance training for runner."
   —**Arthur Lydiard**

◆

"I like hills because you can see the top. I know that sounds glib, but you know that the hill is not going to keep appearing; it's there and once you get to the top it's behind you, and you feel as though you have conquered something."
   —**Rob de Castella**

◆

"Running hills breaks up your rhythm and forces your muscles to adapt to new stresses. The result? You become stronger." —**Eamonn Coghlan**

◆

"I don't go looking for hills, but when I come to one, I run it." —**Jack Mahurin**

◆

"Don't attack a hill from the very bottom—it's bigger than you are!"
　　　　—**Harry Groves**, Penn State coach

◆

"I lean with the hill. . . . I know I'm doing it right if it feels like I'm going to fall on my face, but don't."
　　　　—**Ed Eyestone** on downhill running

◆

"Running up and down a mountain is not just any old 10-K road race. It's an adventure, a taste of excitement; it's a realization that the human body—your body—is a tough old thing. And that you're the boss of it, you can make it do this strange thing—this defying of gravity! Steve Ovett meets Sir Edmund Hillary."
　　　　—**Douglas Barry** on Irish mountain racing

"The biggest hill came at 11 miles, climbing several blocks straight up, only to crest and then free fall for 200 yards to a 90-degree turn. The last mile and a half was flat or slightly downhill. I counted five mortuaries along the way—not a great omen—but at least I'd be well taken care of if the worst occurred."

> —**Ed Eyestone**'s description of the Parkersburg, West Virginia, half-marathon course

◆

"It is suicidal for other runners to copy my hill sessions without adequate background."

> —**Pekka Vasala,** 1972 1500 meter Olympic champ

◆

"If you die, I will bury you in the sandhills with all the other runners."

> —**Percy Cerutty** greeting a visitor to his Portsea training camp

◆

"Someone called the downgrade before Dale Hill the 'Valley of Shattered Dreams.'"

> —**Ted Corbitt,** on the toughest part of the London-to-Brighton ultramarathon

"Somebody said the first one to the top gets a case of beer." —**Rod Dixon,** on climbing Hayes Street Hill in Bay to Breakers

◆

"If the hill has its own name, then it's probably a pretty tough hill."
—**Marty Stern**

◆

HILLS WITH A "NAME"

Agony	(The sand hill at Portsea)
Heartbreak Hill	(Boston Marathon)
Bearcage Hill	(Franklin Park, Boston)
Breakaneck Hill	(Plunging downhill at Mt. SAC)
General Lee's Revenge	(Richmond Marathon)
Capitol Punishment	(In Atlanta, near the state capitol)
Cardiac Hill	(Peachtree 10-K, Atlanta; also, in Sudbury Ontario and Burnaby Mountain, California)
Cemetery Hill	(Van Cortlandt Park, New York)
The Big Dipper	(Sweeping sand hill at Merthyr Mawr, Wales, where Steve Ovett occasionally trained)

Doomsday Hill	(Bloomsday 12-K)
Parachute Hill	(Belmont Plateau Cross-Country Course, Philadelphia)
Surekill Hill	(Belmont Plateau)
Insult	(Dipsea Race, California)
Dynamite	(Dipsea Race. Named for what it does to your quads)
Dead-Horse Hill	(Near Worcester, Massachusetts. So-named in the old days when horses could hardly haul their carts up it)
Out of Breath Hill	(Translation of *Ajoguillo*, in the San Blas Half Marathon, Puerto Rico)
The Bloody Basin Backbreaker	
	(Bloody Basin 50-Miler, Arizona)
The Wall	(Melbourne, Australia . . . And others around the globe as well)
The Black Slink	(Hong Kong)
The Devil's Elbow	(New Zealand)

"The first time I ran it, it was hell. I almost passed out. But I can honestly say this hill has made me a better player. The hill has no weaknesses, and if you consistently beat it, then in your mind you have no weaknesses."

—**Tiki Barber,** New York Giants running back, on the 2 1/2-mile hill run he runs for pre-season conditioning

In the Footsteps of Atalanta
(Women and Running)

"One of the reasons some people don't support women in sport is that through sport we shatter into a million pieces the stereotypes portraying women as weak, helpless, dependent and passive. Through sport we produce exactly the opposite type of woman: strong, independent, assertive, competent and confident, with strong self-esteem."

—**Christine H.B. Grant**, University of Iowa's director of athletics

IN THE FOOTSTEPS OF ATALANTA
(Women and Running)

One of my favorite Greek myths celebrates Atalanta—the fleet-footed huntress who refused to entertain a marriage proposal from any man who couldn't beat her in a race. And no man could. Even Hippomenes, her eventual husband, had to cheat a bit. At crucial times in their footrace, Hippomenes rolled three golden apples off the course. Each time Atalanta veered off to scoop up the gilded enticement—a detour which allowed Hippomenes to stay just one step ahead of the gold-laden maiden at the finish line.

The origin of the Atalanta myth itself might be interesting to know, given that the ancient Greeks banned women from Olympic competition. Mythology aside, women have been trying to even out the playing fields ever since. The issues have covered everything from the right to participate (women didn't run in the Olympics until 1928) to equal prize money in the elite races. For women runners, progress has no doubt seemed as plodding as some of Atalanta's more slow-footed suitors.

Joan Benoit Samuelson's historic entrance into the Los

Angeles Olympic stadium in 1984 was not only glorious; it also served as an exclamation mark on the work of pioneers like Roberta Gibb, Nina Kuscsik, and especially Kathrine Switzer—who had all pushed, directly or indirectly, for a women's Olympic marathon for over a decade.

Now we (male or female) cannot imagine the sport of long distance running with a Joanie, a Grete, or an Uta Pippig. Ultramarathon runners cannot imagine their events without Ann Trason, who has, on occasion, won ultra races, beating *all* the participants, male and female.

But it wasn't that long ago when Olympic bureaucrats deemed that 800 meters was far too dangerous for the fairer sex. When several of the women 800-meter runners in the 1928 Olympics in Amsterdam collapsed in a finish line heap, ignorance charged into the forefront. Doctors lectured in European newspapers to the effect that grueling endurance sports would make women "old too soon." Anti-feminist forces in the Inter-national Amateur Athletic Federation banned women from any race longer than 200 meters—a ruling not rescinded until 1960!

Because sport holds great sway and interest in most

nations, women runners can—and do—effect the social and political structures of a country. When Tegla Loroupe wins the New York City Marathon she becomes a visible role model for young women runners in male-dominated Kenya. When Hassiba Boulemerka wins the Olympic 1500 meters, young women in Algeria gain strength—despite fundamentalist doctrines there which forbid women to show their legs (rather difficult when you're running in 105-degree heat) or even their unveiled faces.

The integration of men and women, girls and boys, has empowered long distance running with a unique quality—an appreciation and respect that crosses the barriers of sexism. Skeptics need only attend a high school or collegiate cross-country meet and, most likely, they'll see what I see: men cheering on women, women cheering on men, or—more accurately—runners supporting other runners. Because we all essentially face the same challenges in running, it's easy to relate. A male football payer and a female field hockey player are not likely to have mutual interest in each other's respective endeavor.

Women runners will take on some of the greatest challenges of long distance running in their approach to the great barrier records. Soon they will shatter the 2:20 mark in the marathon. (Consider that the best women marathoners now run faster than Emil Zatopek did when he set the Olympic record of 2:23 at Helsinki in 1952.) Will women eventually threaten the four-minute mile barrier? One woman running 4:09 would set off a record attempt "rush" such as has not been seen since Bannister and the boys took it down a notch in 1954.

What else can we expect as women's athletics head toward the 21st century? Major leaps in track and field, for one thing. Look for women to become increasingly more visible in two of the most demanding—and potentially exciting—events in Olympic competition. Women are destined to soar in the pole-vault and make a splash in the steeplchase pit. Barriers, in all senses of the word, will be cleared.

"They're very tenacious. They're dedicated. Once a woman decides she's going to do something she'll probably stick to it. The only problem with women is if there's anything wrong with them they won't tell you. They'll get out there and run on one leg. They don't moan and groan like a lot of men do."
   —Arthur Lydiard

◆

"They are beautiful because they run and they run because they are beautiful."
      —Dr. Ernest van Aaken, when asked why
         attractive women run

◆

"I am against the participation of women in public competition. At the Olympic Games their primary role should be like that at the ancient tournaments, the crowning of victors with laurels."
   —Baron Pierre de Coubertin, 1935

◆

"Women are runners by nature, just as men are."
      —Ken Doherty, 1972

◆

"It's the lioness that hunts."
> **—Slogan of a British women's running club**

◆

"We were trying to attract older athletes, and they weren't coming. It wasn't fashionable. So we opened the meets up to little boys. And with little boys competing, it wasn't long before there were little girls."
> **—Bill Bowerman** on starting "all-comer" meets in Eugene back in the 1960s

◆

"I see women and they don't do anything; only men do things. This is the nature of oppression of women in our society; men do, and women just are. I'd rather be one who does—so I run."
> **—Charlotte Lettis,** distance runner, 1972

◆

"In a country where only men are encouraged, one must be one's own inspiration."
> **—Tegla Loroupe,** Kenya, 1994 New York City Marathon champion

◆

"Hassiba [Boulmerka] is our idol. We are in a hostile environment, but she gives us hope."
   —A 16-year-old Algerian girl

◆

"I'm personally not willing to wait 20 years for an Olympic women's marathon, and feel the sooner we make this point, the better our chances are for '76 or at the latest, 1980."
   —Kathrine Switzer

◆

"It was devastating for the lone woman in a marathon not to finish."
         —Nina Kuscsik, who was forced to drop out of
         the NY Marathon because of a virus in 1970.
         She won Boston in 1972

◆

"We need to keep breaking down the myths about what women can't do. It hasn't been that long since women were first allowed to run the marathon in the Olympics. It's important to keep expressing ourselves physically."
         —Ann Bancroft, first woman to reach
         the North Pole

"I thought about how many preconceived prejudices would crumble when I trotted right along for 26 miles."

—**Roberta Gibb**, sculptor, and the first woman to finish the Boston Marathon

"You know, I'm no women's libber, but the media can really irritate me. I sure get tired of being 'pert' Francie Larrieu.' That kind of stuff has to stop. All those ridiculous adjectives they always use with women."

—**Francie Larrieu**, 1975

"I'm not a women's chauvinist. . . Now and then there'll be some guy who'll make some horrid comment that makes me a little bit mad. But basically the guys that we've run with have been very good to us. And I don't think we're doing anything to their egos."

—**Doris Brown Heritage**, 1960s

"The trouble [with most women athletes] is that they do not want to train hard enough. One must practice every day." —**Fanny Blankers-Koen**, Holland, winner of 4 golds in the 1948 London Olympics

"Finally, one man's view on how British women athletes dress. If our girls are behind the rest of the world in athletic prowess, they are certainly well ahead in the scantiness of their running garments. Perhaps I am a bit of a puritan, but I am certainly no prude, and I have been quite shocked sometimes by the display of female form in those flimsy bikini-style briefs and vests. It seems to be unnecessary showing off. And these too-short shorts do not display a woman to advantage, particularly from the back. Sometimes they look downright indecent."

—**Gordon Pirie**, 1961 from *Running Wild*,
a chapter titled "A Bold Word To The Girls"

◆

"A woman naturally thinks about how she looks, and the marathon beats you up so much that you look terrible at the end. You do not happily go before the cameras. You just primp yourself as best you can and tell yourself, well, what can I do about it?"

—**Uta Pippig**

◆

"Joanie, if marathons make you look like this, please don't run any more."

> —**Joan Benoit's mother**, in a letter, after Joan's exhausted face appeared in a newspaper photo upon winning Boston in 2:22:43

◆

"We've fought for equality, and now we have to face the responsibility of getting exhausted in public."

> —**Kathrine Switzer**

◆

"Our headmistress told us not to run cross-country or we'd end up looking like Russian shot putters. . . I started measuring my legs every day to see if they were getting too muscular. I decided that when they increased above a certain size I'd stop running."

> —**Lorraine Moller**, 1992 bronze marathon medalist, on beginning to run as a schoolgirl in New Zealand

◆

"To convince myself that creating more women's running opportunities, as I'm doing right now, is more important than dreaming about, "What if I got in good shape again?'"

— **Kathrine Switzer**, 1980 New Year's resolution

◆

"Women have never raced like men before. They've never gone 'all out' so they collapse at the end. They always manage to jog back to hotel rooms a mile or two right after the finish. They recover too fast. Here—this time—Marty's going to run against the edge of death."

— **Brian Oldfield**, Marty Cooksey's coach, prior to her 1978 NYC Marathon. She placed second in 2:41:49 behind Grete Waitz's world record of 2:32:30.

◆

"Some newspapers wrote stories about this crazy doctor who was trying to train Emil Zatopeks in pigtails. . . . They thought my license to practice medicine should be revoked."

— **Dr. Ernest van Aaken**, German coach who promoted women's running in the late 60s and early 70s

"You are foolish to put a little girl in the marathon."

   —**Portuguese officials** to Jose Pedrosa prior to Rosa Mota's winning of her first of three European Marathon Championships

◆

"If this race is for 'men only,' why doesn't it *say* 'men only' on the entry blank?"

   —**Nina Kuscsik**, 1969

◆

"I'm not prejudiced against women; they just can't run in my race!"

   —**Jock Semple**, Boston Athletic Association official on why he tried to prevent Kathrine Switzer from running the Boston Marathon

◆

"I don't want to run with the boys. It's stupid. Even though I know that I can beat most of the boys my age, that doesn't help the other girls very much. I'd rather see our school have a girls' cross-country team separate from the boys, but I don't think they ever will."

   —**Mary Decker**, age 15

◆

"Twice we were told that she was about to become the first Irish woman athlete to win a European gold. Well, yes. . . But then again, no. She's the first Irish athlete, full stop, to win a European championship. Eventually, we'll all just have to get used to the idea of a woman as the most successful Irish sports person of the age and the most successful Irish athlete ever."

> —**Eamonn McCann**, concerning a radio broadcast describing Sonia O'Sullivan's 1994 European 3000-meter championship

◆

"They meant, of course, the first American *man*, so they should say so."

> —**Doris Brown Heritage**, on hearing Craig Virgin described as "the first American" to win a World Cross-Country title. She had won five.

◆

"[Women's marathon] behavior is accepted and even admired. And that should never be taken for granted. I can remember when I used to get up at five in the morning to go out running, and I couldn't even find a dog to run with me."

> —**Toshiko D'Elia**, 3rd in the 1976 NYC Marathon at age 46

"The biggest change is the mass social acceptance. People used to think I was a freak. Now women of all shapes and sizes run all the time. And they're not just beautiful and slim and wearing pink gossamer tights. They jiggle along at 12-minute miles or spring along at 6:30s. And everyone just ignores them because they're part of the landscape. That's what I love."

—**Kathrine Switzer**

◆

"No one could have scripted a more celebratory inauguration of the new era than Benoit's victory and the great race she led. . . . A woman was enabled to achieve what Benoit accomplished. A woman was welcomed in that achievement by a roar of acclamation that was unequalled for any male through the whole Games. Women competed with each other to the absolute rigorous limit of their will. And a woman endured utter exhaustion in the sight of millions of people—because she chose to do so. I have been astonished that so few feminists outside the USA seemed awake enough to fanfare the magnitude of what was achieved that day."

—**Roger Robinson**, *Heroes and Sparrows*

◆

"Once I was out for a twenty-miler on the grass along the Parkway, but I was picked up by the police after three miles. It was raining and someone called and told them 'There's a crazy woman running. . . .' They took me and left me off at the next exit."

      —**Nina Kuscsik,** on running in the 1960s

◆

"I see myself as an artist. Running is the way I express my talent. I wish I could paint or write music, but running is what I do and I feel great joy from it."

      —**Joan Nesbit,** world-class runner

◆

"In the 1970s, the respected German coach Manfred Steffney said that a woman would never break 2:30 for the marathon. Now we laugh at him."

      —**Dr. David Martin,** sports physiologist

◆

"I read in *Cosmo* that women reach their peak at forty, so I still have five years."

      —**Regina Jacobs,** after winning the Fifth
        Avenue Mile

The Marathon

At Marathon arrayed, to the battle shock we ran

And our mettle we displayed, foot to foot, man to
man

And our name and fame shall not die.

—**Aristophanes**, "The Acharnians," 425 B.C.

THE MARATHON

While compiling this book, it occurred to me that ninety percent of the material in the "Marathon" section could have served equally well in the "Pain" section. Such is the nature of the race. Maybe the worst part about the marathon is the *knowing* that pain will come; the *thinking* about it, more than the actual pain itself. You are like a boxer, slumped in the corner between rounds, knowing that no longer can you hold up your arms to block the inevitable jabs and round-house rights. Of course, you can step off the course, but there's a lot of mental anguish involved in such a step—enough that I am not sure whether it is an act of cowardice or courage to drop out of a marathon.

Then there was the time in New York, where, in the space of one thousand meters, I went from feeling great (running 2:20 pace and thinking: "Why didn't I go out faster?"), to—as Farrington describes it so well in this section—as if I had cut myself, and every ounce of emotional and physical energy, inexplicably and horrificly, was seeping out onto the cold, gray road in the Bronx in front of people that I did not know.

A block or two later there was the New York cop—walrus-like mustache, walkie-talkie squawking on his belt—who took one quick glance at this face without spirit, this sorry shuffler, and softly said, a voice laced with sympathy: "Pretty tough day to try and be a hero, kid."

And, in Harlem, the man who got in my face (thank God) and got me going again with: "Yo, man! Whatch you doin'? I didn't come out here to watch you *walk*!" And so I began to trot again, pounding my way through Central Park—walking again until I could not stand the shame of it; trotting again—a weaving obstacle to those around me diligently racing toward their sub-2:50's.

"The marathon," Bill Rodgers once said, "can humble you."

But the marathon can exhilarate, too. Isn't that the lure? Isn't that what brings us back when, as Shorter says, we've managed to *forget* about the last one?

"Men, today we die a little."
>   —**Emil Zatopek,** on the starting line for the
>   Olympic Marathon

◆

"To describe the agony of a marathon to someone who's never run it is like trying to explain color to someone who was born blind."
>   —**Jerome Drayton**

◆

"In this mechanized society of ours, marathoners want to assert their independence and affirm their individuality more than ever. Call it humanism, call it health, call it folly. Some are Lancelots, some are Don Quixotes. All are noble."
>   —**Erich Segal**

◆

"The marathon is a charismatic event. It has everything. It has drama. It has competition. It has camaraderie. It has heroism. Every jogger can't dream of being an Olympic champion, but he can dream of finishing a marathon."
>   —**Fred Lebow**

"The marathon, you see, is my benchmark. It is the status symbol in my community, the running community."

—Dr. George Sheehan

"The marathon is like a bullfight. There are two ways to kill a bull, for instance. There is the easy way, for one. But all the great matadors end up either dead or mauled because for them killing the bull is not nearly as important as *how* they kill the bull. They always approach the bull at the greatest risk to themselves, and I admire that. In the marathon, likewise, there are two ways to win. There's the easy way if all you care about is winning. You hang back and risk nothing. Then kick and try to nip the leaders at the end. Or you can push, challenge the others, make it an exciting race, risking everything. Maybe you lose, but as for me, I'd rather run a gutsy race, pushing all the way and lose, then run a conservative, easy race only for a win."

—Alberto Salazar, 1981

"God! He's running backwards!"

—Words of the broadcaster who witnessed Jim Peters' collapse in the Empire Games Marathon of 1954

"The miler knows that in just over four minutes the pain of severe effort will subside. . . . But the marathoner must be able to tolerate pain and fatigue for over two hours."
         —**Buddy Edelen,** 1964

◆

"If you feel bad at ten miles, you're in trouble. It you feel bad at twenty miles you're normal. If you don't feel bad at twenty-six miles, you're abnormal."
         —**Rob de Castella**

◆

"Why couldn't Pheidippides have died here?"
         —**Frank Shorter**'s comment to Kenny Moore at the sixteen-mile mark in one of Shorter's first marathons

◆

"Marathon running is a terrible experience—monotonous, heavy, and exhausting."
         —**Veikko Karvonen,** 1954 European and Boston Marathon champ

◆

"You have to forget your last marathon before you try another. Your mind can't know what's coming."
         —**Frank Shorter**

"Marathoning is like cutting yourself unexpectedly. You dip into the pain so gradually that the damage is done before you are aware of it. Unfortunately, when awareness comes, it is excruciating."
　　—John Farrington, Australian marathoner

◆

"There is the truth about the marathon and very few of you have written the truth. . . . Even if I explain to you, you'll never understand it, you're outside of it."
　　—Douglas Wakiihuri speaking to journalists

◆

"We are different, in essence, from other men. If you want to win something, run 100 meters. If you want to experience something, run a marathon."
　　—Emil Zatopek

◆

"I definitely want to show how beautiful the marathon can be. I am the opponent of all those who find the marathon bad: the psychologists, the physiologists, the doubters. I make the marathon beautiful for myself and for others. That's why I'm here."
　　—Uta Pippig

◆

"I said to myself, 'If this is the marathon, it's no problem.' . . . . That's the only marathon I've ever said that about."
>—**Gelindo Bordin**, recalling his comfortable
>2:13:20 debut win at Milan Marathon in 1984

◆

"I felt like I played in a very rough football game with no hitting above the waist."
>—**Alan Page,** former NFL football star

◆

"I used to rehearse the marathon in the last few miles of every long training run. It was not particularly pleasant for my training partners."
>—**Pete Pfitzinger,** two-time U.S. Olympian

◆

"Three hours slow is better than two hours fast."
>—**Pete Gavuzzi,** Gerard Cote's marathon coach
>in the 1940s, on how to train

◆

"You can actually suffer a little bit more going slowly than when you're going really fast. A faster marathon might even be easier than a slow one, in terms of what it takes out of you mentally."
>—**Frank Shorter**

"At the two-thirds mark, I think of those who are still with me. Who might make a break? Should I? Then I give it all I've got."

—**Ibrahim Hussein,** on marathon tactics

◆

"The marathon's about being in contention over the last 10K. That's when it's about what you have in your core. You have run all the strength, all the superficial fitness out of yourself, and it really comes down to what's left inside *you*. To be able to draw deep and pull something out of yourself is one of the most tremendous things about the marathon."

—**Rob de Castella**

◆

In 1968, **George Young** ran the Olympic Trials Marathon as insurance—in case he didn't make the U.S. team in the steeplechase. Asked if he expected to better his time when he ran the marathon again, he said: "Anybody who runs more than one of these is nuts."

◆

"I'm never going to run another marathon."

—**Oprah Winfrey**

◆

"I'm not going to run this again."
>—**Grete Waitz** after winning her *first* of nine
>New York City Marathons

◆

"Despite the sun and the caution it should have instilled in me, I wanted to prove the course wasn't as tough as they said, the heat wasn't that bad. But by 22 miles I got the whoozies and pretty soon I'm sitting on a rock, and the next thing I know I'm in the car. Fifteen minutes pass, and Nick Costes walks up to the car and climbs in. So these two heroes are out. We sit there like melted butter. Ted Corbitt just trudged along and won with a 2:46:13. Only forgetfulness and the indestructibility of youth brought me back to that race again."
>—**Johnny J. "Young John" Kelley**, on his first
>attempt at the Yonkers Marathon, 1954

◆

"The marathon can humble you."
>—**Bill Rodgers**

◆

"I am too tired, even to be happy."
>—**Gelindo Bordin**, Italy, immediately after
>winning the Olympic Marathon in Seoul

"I was unable to walk for a whole week after that, so much did the race take out of me. But it was the most pleasant exhaustion I have ever known."

> —**Emil Zatopek**'s description of the Olympic Marathon win in Helsinki

◆

1. THE BOSTON MARATHON

"The Boston Marathon, America's greatest footrace, 2,000 Walter Mittys bucking for flat feet and a heart attack. . . . For most, it's the Boston Massacre."

> —**Jim Murray**, *Los Angeles Times* sports columnist

◆

"The event that certainly tries men's soles."

> —**Jerry Nason**, Boston sportswriter, 1945

◆

"The Boston Marathon has had more to do with liberating and promoting women's marathoning than any other race in the world."

> —**Joe Henderson**

"Run even splits! Very few runners have run fast on this course without running even splits. Unless your name is Joan Benoit, you can't throw out the rule book: Joan went through 10 miles in 51:38 when she set the record back in '83. . . But that's Joanie."

> —**Bob Sevene**, coach, on "How to run the
> Boston Marathon course"

◆

"Give it hell down the hills! Give it hell down the hills!"

> —**Jock Semple** to Amby Burfoot, en route to
> his 1968 win

◆

"Get going. Get up and walk if you have to, but finish the damned race."

> —**Ron Hill** to Jerome Drayton during the 1970
> Boston Marathon

◆

"I saw the Prudential Center Tower from about two miles out, but for quite a while I thought it was a mirage. I kept seeing it and seeing it and I thought I'd never get there."

> —**Neil Cusack**, Ireland, 1974 winner who
> muttered, "Thank God, it's over!" when
> he finished

"By a fillip of testing fate, I bore the monarch's name."
>—**John J. "Young John" Kelley**, Boston
>Marathon Champ, 1957

◆

2. THE NEW YORK CITY MARATHON

"To believe this story you must believe that the human race can be one joyous family, working together, laughing together, achieving the impossible. I believe it because I saw it happen. Last Sunday, in one of the most violent, trouble-stricken cities in the world, 12,000 men, women, and children from 40 countries of the world, assisted by 2.5-millon black, white, and yellow people, Protestants and Catholics, Jews and Muslims, Buddhists and Confucians, laughed, cheered, and suffered during the greatest folk festival the world has seen."
>—**Chris Brasher**, after the 1979 NYC Marathon.
>Brasher was so inspired he became Director of
>the London Marathon.

◆

"The New York Marathon—a fantastic event."
>—**Pope John Paul II**, 1982

"The starting line of the New York City Marathon is kind of like a giant time bomb behind you about to go off. It is the most spectacular start in sport."

—Bill Rodgers, as a TV commentator, 1987

◆

"The best sporting event in the country is the New York City Marathon because people embrace that event."

—Peter Ueberroth

◆

"There are people who are visionaries and people who are bookkeepers. Fred [Lebow] brought running up center stage. He's done radical things and he's made mistakes. But you need people with imagination and Fred has it." **—Norman Goluskin**, Central Park Track Club

◆

"In 1979, everybody false started. They went before the gun. I had no idea. Jon Anderson, Ron Hill, Bill Rodgers, we all stood there. I said: 'One of the four of us had better win this because the rest should be disqualified.'"

—Kenny Moore

◆

"I'm not going to stand at the start of the race on the Verrazano Narrows Bridge and get peed on."

—**Don Imus** of WFAN's "Imus in the Morning"
on why he won't run the NYC Marathon

"When I came to New York in 1978, I was a full-time schoolteacher and track runner, and determined to retire from competitive running. But winning the New York City Marathon kept me running for another decade."

—**Grete Waitz**

"That win ten years ago was the topping off of my whole career. New York is the one you have to win."

—**Rod Dixon**, 1993

"I never felt as bad as I did over those last two miles. It was like running with a hangover. Like having gone out and partied yourself to death and trying to get up the next morning."

—**Geoff Smith**, runnerup in 1983's epic battle

"When you run up First Avenue in New York, if you don't get goose bumps, there's something wrong with you."
—**Frank Shorter**

◆

"The first time through the five boroughs was so unexpected. I'm from Oregon, I hate New York, every day except Marathon Sunday. The kids slapping hands with you, saying, 'Way to go, honky!' I love that."
—**Kenny Moore**

◆

"It would mean more for me to win in New York than to come back and do another Olympic marathon."
—**Joan Benoit Samuelson**, 1991

◆

"The last six miles were a struggle. If it weren't for the crowds and the fact that it is the New York City Marathon, I don't know if I would have finished. Besides, I heard if you try and stop, the crowds won't let you."
—**Grete Waitz** in 1985, after her 7th NYC win

◆

"If I'd known New York was going to be such a big deal, I'd have won it six times."
—**Tom Fleming,** NYC champ in 1973 and 1975

The Mile

"Après moi le deluge."

—**Sir Roger Bannister,** after running history's first sub-four-minute mile

THE MILE

In junior high school, I discovered a book in the library. It was *The Four Minute Mile,* written by Roger Bannister. I loved that book. The words and pictures held me like a spell. I read it virtually every time my class went to the library. I felt like it was *my* book.

Soon after, I ran my first timed mile in gym class. I remember I ran it in socks because—instinctively—I must have figured the clunky black high top basketball sneakers would hinder my slight, hundred-pound frame in its objective of covering four laps around the hilltop oval. The cinders ripped up my once-white socks, leaving two round holes—rimmed in a sooty, black-gray, as if someone had taken a gun and blasted each at close range and left the tell-tale powderburns. I ran 6:04—and I was really proud of that. Later I heard Doug Byren, a tall, rangy star on the soccer team, had clocked 5:56 in the other gym class and I was, as we said back then, kind of bummed out. Years later, in an indoor college meet, I placed second in a mile race. Two watches read 4:20.0, but I searched for—and found—one guy (*not* a relative. . . .) who had me in 4:19.9, and I now claim that (rightly or wrongly) as my mile PR.

The mile was always good for a pre-race avalanche of adrenalin. There's a certain urgency to the mile, which requires both the explosiveness of the sprints and the endurance of the longer races. The starter bids you to take your marks, your heart is pounding in your ribcage like some small animal trying to get out, and every muscle is on the verge of involuntary convulsion.

A well-run mile can have a unique hum to it, a rhythmic flow of perfectly paced quarters. But miles can hold a kind of captivating violence, too, with make-or- break third lap bids from the strength runners and do-or-die surges from the kickers that sweep ferociously off the final turn in flashes of color and churning limbs. And is there a better definition of hell than receiving a ten-yard lead when you're running the mile anchor leg of a highly-competitive distance medley relay? I think not.

Good miles are somewhat rare. And great miles—truly great miles—are works of art that can never be precisely duplicated.

"The man who made the mile record is W. G. George. . . . His time was 4 minutes, 12.75 seconds and the probability is that this record will never be beaten."
—**Harry Andrews**, 1903

◆

"The mile has all the elements of drama."
—**Sir Roger Bannister**

◆

"The mile has a classic symmetry. . . . It's a play in four acts."   —**John Landy**

◆

"Blink and you miss a sprint. The 10,000 meters is lap after lap of waiting. Theatrically, the mile is just the right length—beginning, middle, end, a story unfolding."
—**Sebastian Coe**

◆

"It's a brick wall. I shall not attempt it again."
—**John Landy**, after running between 4:02 and 4:03 six times in 1953

◆

"If ever we [he and Hägg] would get together and help each other, the 4-minute mile would be ours for the asking."   —**Arne Andersson**

◆

"Whether as athletes we liked it or not, the 4-minute mile had become rather like an Everest—a challenge to the human spirit, it was a barrier that seemed to defy all attempts to break it—an irksome reminder that man's striving might be in vain."
     —**Sir Roger Bannister**

◆

"I think it's bloody silly to put flowers on the grave of the 4-minute mile, now isn't it? It turns out it wasn't so much like Everest as it was like the Matterhorn; somebody had to climb it first, but I hear now they've even got a cow up it."
     —**Harry Wilson**, coach

◆

"Popular myth says it was Roger Bannister. Unfortunately, for accuracy's sake, this is not true. Roger ran 3:59.4 in that historic race, which, of course, is faster than 4:00. History has little noted, nor long remembered Derek Ibbotson, the man who first ran 4:00.0."
     —**Jerry McFadden**, writer/runner

"How did I know you ran a 4:30 mile in high school? That's easy. *Everyone* ran a 4:30 mile in high school."
>   —**Frank Shorter**, circa 1969, from
>   *Once A Runner*, quote preceding Chapter 1

◆

"There was nothing unusual about my victory. The entire story was back in eighth place. There is simply no way to imagine how good Jim Ryun is or how far he will go after he becomes an adult. What he did was more significant than Roger Bannister's first mile under 4 minutes."
>   —**Jim Burleson**, after winning the Compton
>   Invitational Mile on June 5, 1964. Ryun,
>   just 17, ran 3:59.0

◆

"I ran my first sub-4-minute mile in 1977 and since then have run 136 more. Nobody has run as many sub-4s as I have, and I intend to run at least one more."
>   —**Steve Scott**, 1995, after cancer surgery

◆

"The 800-meter record, the records in the 1,000, the 1,500, the 5,000, the relays—no one remembers them. The mile, they remember. Only the mile."
>   —**John Walker**

"Almost every part of the mile is tactically important—you can never let down, never stop thinking, and you can be beaten at almost any point. I suppose you could say it is like life."

  —John Landy

◆

"Roger Bannister studied the four-minute mile the way Jonas Salk studied polio—with a view to eradicating."

  —Jim Murray, *L. A. Times* columnist

◆

"When you hear the crowd noise, it means that little bastard has made his move."

  —John Walker's alleged comment about
    Eammon Coghlan, complimenting his skill
    at indoor mile racing

◆

"I've been in more 4:01 to 4:03 races than I care to remember. My career as a runner won't be complete unless I can join that exclussive club."

  —Jason Stewart, U.S. Army captain, on trying
    to go sub-4

"My race only takes about four minutes, but the difference I can make for other people lasts much longer than that."
—**Marla Runyan,** legally-blind runner who serves as an inspiration to many. Runyan made the Olympic 1500 finals in Sydney.

Mind Over Matter

"Now if you are going to win any battle you have to do one thing. You have to make the mind run the body. Never let the body tell the mind what to do. The body will always give up. It is always tired morning, noon, and night. But the body is never tired if the mind is not tired. When you were younger the mind could make you dance all night, and the body was never tired. . . .You've always got to make the mind take over and keep going."

      —**George S. Patton**, U. S. Army General
        and 1912 Olympian

MIND OVER MATTER

Perhaps one of the most famous verbal exchanges in the history of running occurred in the 1952 Olympic Marathon in Helsinki between Emil Zatopek—the Czech making his debut at the 26.2 mile distance—and the world recordholder Jim Peters of England.

Zatopek, already the winner in the 10,000 and 5000 meter races, and pursuing an unparalleled distance triple, pulled up to the fast-starting Peters around 15K. Peters, who had run a world record marathon of 2:20:42 just six weeks prior to the Olympic Games, was already feeling the strain of the race—but trying his best not to show it.

"The pace, Jim, is it too fast?" asked Zatopek, the supposed novice.

Peters snapped back: "No, the pace is too slow!" Whereupon the Englishman surged ahead. But Zatopek went with Peters, took control of the race by halfway and eventually pulled away to an Olympic record win of 2:23:03. This story is usually told in a way that suggests that Zatopek—being new to the marathon—truly was asking for guidance from Peters. But I'm not so sure. I've always felt Zatopek was exercising a bit of mental gamemanship; it was his way of telling Peters, "Hey, I'm right here—and I feel pretty good."

Sometimes it's better not to know *everything* about an opponent. New Zealand's Rod Dixon (a former world-class miler) spent most of the latter stages of the 1983 New York City Marathon chasing down Geoff Smith. All the while, Dixon thought: "Why should a marathoner beat a miler?" and tried to keep Smith in sight. Dixon kept repeating to himself, as if it were some magical mantra: "A miler's kick does the trick. . . A miler's kick does the trick. . . "

Finally, Dixon hauled Smith in over the last half-mile and won one of the most famous marathon duels in history. In fact, Smith had a sub-four-minute mile on his resume, too, but Dixon had't known this en route to his memorable victory.

The great Herb Elliott, world record setter and gold medalist in the 1500 at Rome, tells the story of practicing on the same track with Australia's second best miler, Merv Lincoln. It was a very windy day, and Lincoln was running his sprints with the wind at his back. But Elliott, who prided himself on mental and physical toughness, was running his speed session *into* the teeth of the gale.

"I knew then," Elliott said, "that he would never beat me."

And Elliott never did lose to Lincoln, though Lincoln did run the same time as Elliott in one race—Elliott gaining the official win in the "photo-finish" by an inch. Some say Elliott was physically the better runner. But a case can be made for the awesome power of self-confidence, focus, and determination.

" "

"Mind is everything: muscle—pieces of rubber. All that I am, I am because of my mind."
   —Paavo Nurmi

◆

"I don't know about psychology; I'm a runner."
   —Steve Jones, when asked about his thought
      process after breaking the world record in
      the marathon in 1984

◆

"Running is my meditation, mind flush, cosmic telephone, mood elevator and spiritual communion."
　—Lorraine Moller

◆

"The five S's of sports training are: stamina, speed, strength, skill, and spirit; but the greatest of these is spirit."
　—Ken Doherty

◆

"In my 1976 Training Diary is a photo of Jack Nicholson from *One Flew Over The Cuckoo's Nest*. It's a facial shot of him trying to pull out the drinking trough and use it to smash one of the barred windows to escape. One of the other patients said: 'Don't be stupid, you can't do that.' Jack replied, 'Yes I can, anything is possible.' He strained his guts working at it for a few minutes with the veins sticking out of his neck. Of course he couldn't move the bloody thing. They all said: 'We told you that you couldn't do it.' Nicholson looked at them and said: 'At least I tried, you bastards.' To me that summarizes what I think about life."
　—Chris Wardlaw, 2:11 Australian marathoner

◆

"Run hard, be strong, think big!"
  —Percy Cerutty

◆

"On Saturday night, I said to myself, 'Are you ready to deal with a victory?' I decided I was."
  —Joan Benoit on her thoughts prior to the
  1984 Olympic Marathon

◆

"The difference between my world record and many world class runners is mental fortitude. I ran believing in mind over matter."
  —Derek Clayton

◆

"A lot of people run a race to see who's the fastest. I run to see who has the most guts."
  —Steve Prefontaine

◆

"Part of a runner's training consists of pushing back the limits of his mind, of proving to his doubting intellect that sixty-six seconds a lap for twelve laps won't reduce him to another cinder on the track."
  —Kenny Moore

"Last year I ran with her for eleven miles, and I looked across at this woman they made a statue of in Oslo, and I was thinking: 'Wow!' I thought about it afterwards, and you have to knock people off pedestals before you can beat them."

    —**Lisa Martin**, 1986 on Grete Waitz

◆

"It was a wonderful feeling when I came alongside. I glanced at Shorter as I did so, and looked right into the eyes of a man who was my idol as a marathon runner. I knew all about him. And yet I could tell by his return glance that he didn't know much, if anything, about me. The psychological advantage was mine."

    —**Waldemar Cierpinski** on his Olympic victory
      in Montreal

◆

"The great thing about athletics is that it's like poker sometimes: you know what's in your hand and it may be a load of rubbish, but you've got to keep up the front."

    —**Sebastian Coe**

◆

"Once you're beat mentally, you might as well not even go to the starting line."
—**Todd Williams**

◆

"Bob does well in big races because he doesn't stand at the starting line and establish a pecking order. He doesn't look around and say: 'Oh, so-and-so is here. . . .' His great gift is his ability to focus completely on himself and his *own* race, and then let the place or the time take care of itself."
—Coach **Vince Lananna** on Bob Kempainen

◆

"Great job. . . And now, get your head ready to run under 13:00."
—Coach **Sam Bell** to Bob Kennedy after his PR of 13:02

◆

"God has given me the ability. The rest is up to me. Believe. Believe. Believe. . . "
—**Billy Mills,** an entry in his training diary prior to his upset Olympic gold medal 10,000-meter win in Tokyo Olympics

"The body does not want you to do this. As you run, it tells you to stop but the mind must be strong. You always go too far for your body. You must handle the pain with strategy . . . . It is not age; it is not diet. It is the will to succeed."

> —**Jacqueline Gareau**, 1980 Boston Marathon champ

◆

"Concentrate! You're alone but you're not finished. You're alone because you earned it. You can do this and they can't. You are one tough bastard. Say that over again and say it slow. Say it one word at a time. You, are, one, tough, bastard. I love these moments of congratulation. You are a stupid sod. Just keep running and save the back patting for later."

> —**Frank Murphy**, *A Cold Clear Day*: the inner thoughts of Buddy Edelen en route to winning the 1964 Olympic Marathon Trials

◆

"They have a word in Finnish called *sisu*, which basically means guts. It's the strongest word in the Finnish language. You tell a Finn he doesn't have sisu, that's like spitting in his face."

> —**Arthur Lydiard**

"Mental will is a muscle that needs exercise, just like muscles of the body."
　　—Lynn Jennings

◆

"The human body can do so much. Then the heart and spirit must take over."
　　—Sohn Kee-chung, Korean, who won the 1936 Olympic Marathon in Olympic Record time of 2:29:19.2, but was forced to run for Japan

◆

"I remember I was tested out in Eugene, Oregon, by Jack Daniels on the treadmill, and, boy, the results were not good. I can't remember exactly what they were but I had a low VO_2 max, I was low on everything, except two things, Jack said: I was very efficient in my running—I didn't use a whole lot of energy in my run—and the other thing he said was, 'Well, you can't measure what's between the shoulders.'"
　　—Brian Diemer, Olympic bronze medal steeple-chaser in 1984

◆

"[Scientific testing] can't determine how the mind will tolerate pain in a race. Sometimes, I say, 'Today I can die.'" —**Gelindo Bordin**

◆

Someone once asked **Jim Spivey** about what it takes to be a great miler. He measured the distance from his chin to the top of his head with his hands, explaining: "You have to believe what Sebastian Coe says: 'The eight inches right here; set it straight and you can beat anybody in the world.'"

◆

"Running is in my blood—the adrenaline flows before the races, the love/hate of butterflies in your stomach."
>—**Marcus O'Sullivan,** world-class miler and
>Villanova coach

◆

"In the days of my victory and joy I had faith enough to thank the Lord. Now, as well, I should not but accept my accident in grace."
>—**Abebe Bikila,** two-time Olympic marathon
>champion, crippled in a car crash in 1969

"Exercise and a fighting attitude are what people like us need to really live, not the sedentary life most doctors would have us adopt."

> —**Jerry Leith,** who ran a thirteen-mile trail race just six months after a hip replacement operation

◆

"Marathoning is just another form of insanity."

> —**John J. Kelley,** winner of the 1952 Boston Marathon

◆

"Running turns any open place into my chapel. The hour I spend each day as an ascetic, short of water and feeling the slight discomfort of genuine effort, provides me with the strength to know that I can live with less than the world would have me believe."

—**Dean Ottati,** *The Runner and the Path*

The International Runner

We few, we happy few, we band of brothers
For he who sheds his blood with me today
Shall be my brother.

—Shakespeare, *Henry V*

THE INTERNATIONAL RUNNER
(Descriptions, Glimpses and Nicknames
of the Elite and Near-Elite)

When Spiridon Louis approached the stadium for the finish of the 1896 Olympic Marathon in Athens the crowd of 100,000 was already buzzing with the news (delivered by messengers on horseback preceding the leaders) and responded with shouts of "Elleen! Elleen!" ("A Greek! A Greek!").

Which seems only natural. Great runners will always reflect upon their country, region, state or city. Removing national flags and national uniforms will do little to change that fact, though occasionally you hear such a suggestions offered as a remedy to rampant displays of nationalism in international competitions.

Rarely, an athlete becomes so great that he or she can transcend nationalism, and, in effect, become something of a "citizen of the world." Perhaps Emil Zatopek, Kip Keino, and Grete Waitz enjoyed such a status. Based on accomplishment alone, the great Nurmi of Finland *could have* risen to such heights—but his character was cold and inaccessible, even to most of his countrymen.

Sometimes world dominance comes in waves—but it is hard to envision Britain trotting out the likes of Sebastian Coe, Steve Ovett and Steve Cram all in the same decade again. (In fact, so dominant were the British in the middle distances that a young Cram—whose mother was German-born—was said to have considered applying for West German citizenship at an early stage in his career in order to gain a more reasonable chance to make an Olympic team! He opted not to.) East and North African runners are dominating the middle and long distance races as we approach the year 2000, having surpassed the former world leaders such as Great Britain, the United States, New Zealand, and Finland. Who will come next is unknowable. Nations can bring forth a generation of champions with little warning.

Consider 1964, just before the Tokyo Olympics. Australia's Ron Clarke and England's Chris Brasher were discussing the chances of the Americans. The Englishman, who had won the steeplechase gold at Melbourne in '56 and helped pace Bannister to history's first sub-4 minute mile in '54, didn't fancy the Americans for the least bit of success. Said Brasher to Clarke: "Not in a lifetime, old boy, not in a lifetime. . . . The Americans will never win a gold medal in an Olympic distance event. They have got no tradition in their running."

The Americans, in fact, struck two golds. Billy Mills galloped home in the now-epic 10,000 meter run, considered by many as one of the biggest upsets in Olympic history; and the 5000 meter run was won by Bob Schul (with future Oregon coach Bill Dellinger grabbing the bronze.) Eight years later, Frank Shorter landed the gold in the marathon at Munich.

Nationalism, for all its supposed negative effects, arguably fuels progress in terms of results. The Eastern Bloc medal onslaughts of the 1970s, for example, were at least partly a result of the Cold War with the West. More recently, consider the Mexican-African rivalries in road racing, or the Kenyan-Ethiopian (or Kenyan-Moroccan) rivalries in both cross-country and track.

A good example of such intense competition emerged early in the summer of '95. When Ethiopia's Haile Gebresilasie set a new world record in the 10,000 meters (26:43, breaking the mark of Kenya's William Sigei), a couple of Kenyans—Moses Kiptanui and Daniel Komen—roared back to both break Gebresilasie's 5000 meter record a few nights later. Kiptanui (first in 12:55) quickly noted that the Kenyans meant to avenge the "loss" of the 10,000 meter record by taking the Ethiopian's mark in the 5000.

"The 10,000 meters is a Kenyan race," Kiptanui declared. "I was not going to stand anybody from another country encroaching on our zone." And yet some other nation *will* encroach, inevitably, and records will fall.

"

"I don't run to be regarded as anything by anybody. I don't care whether people think I'm the greatest runner ever or the greatest bum ever. I don't run for other people; I don't run for my country. I'm not very nationalistic. Derek Clayton comes first in my book."
 —Derek Clayton

◆

"I run for the Cuban people. I run for the Revolution. I don't run for myself; I can't run for myself. I come from a poor people; my family was very poor."
 —Alberto Juantorena, who won Olympic golds
 at Montreal in both the 400 and 800 meters

"I ran for myself, not Finland."
   —Paavo Nurmi

◆

"It was most important to see the Brazilian flag go up."
   —Joaquim Cruz, after winning the 800
      Olympic gold in L.A.

◆

"You could never get to talk to Nurmi. You could talk to the president of Finland, but not to Nurmi. He was a god. He was above the president."
   —Arthur Lydiard

◆

"It is hazardous to be the top sportsman in Finland. If you do well, you are treated like a king. If you fail, people wish you'd go to hell."
   —Lasse Viren, 1973

◆

"I can't understand how a guy can run so poorly between Olympics, and run so well at the Games. You have to give it to the guy. He must have some ability, but I think there's more to it than reindeer milk."
   —Rod Dixon, on Lasse Viren

"Let me tell you, Lasse Viren doesn't have to blood dope. Maybe the people he beats will have to do something, but not Lasse Viren. I've known him since he was 17, and he's simply the greatest distance runner in the world. But you see, Lasse Viren has four Olympic gold medals around his neck. The other runners only have excuses. That includes both Americans and New Zealanders, who have accused him of having some secret weapon. His secret is fine talent and hard training."

—Arthur Lydiard

◆

"Chris Brasher, Chris Chataway and I, all of us at Oxford University, seemed more privileged than we actually were. We were labeled young 'Elizabethans,' possessing more than a touch of single-mindedness, optimism, and that now unfashionable quality, patriotism."

—Sir Roger Bannister

◆

"If people think I'm an arrogant SOB for doing things my own way, then that's what I am. But I'll still do it. I'm patriotic in my own way. Press my doorbell and it rings: 'Rule Britannia.'"

—Steve Ovett, BBC television interview

"When I was a kid, people would ask if I wanted to be the next Ronny Delany of Ireland, and I said, 'No, I don't want to be Ronny Delany, I want to be the next Eamonn Coghlan of Ireland.'"

> **—Eamonn Coghlan**

◆

"A V-8 engine on a VW frame. . . . He'll destroy so many hearts, they'll all wish they weren't born in his era. What a tough bastard."

> **—John Walker,** description of Noureddine
> Morceli of Algeria

◆

"A being from another world."

> **—Michel Jazy** describing Herb Elliott

◆

Gazalla ed aquila
Il silenzio
dell'altopiano
Il boato all stadio
("Gazelle and eagle/The silence/The plateau/The cheering in the stadium. . . ")

> —Italian poet **Aldo Rossi,** on Abebe Bikila

"We forget our bodies to the benefit of mechanical leisure. We act continuously with our brain, but we no longer use our bodies, our limbs. It is the Africans who possess this vitality, this muscular youth, this thirst for physical action which we are lacking. We have a magnificent motor at our disposal, but we no longer know how to use it."
   —Emil Zatopek

◆

"Being a Kenyan or Japanese doesn't make any difference. It's attitude. What do you want? Maybe I have the talent. Maybe there are things I don't have that I would like to get. By combining two cultures, I can get something that is worthy."
   —Douglas Wakiihuri

◆

"He [Wakiihuri] has the legs of a Kenyan and the mind of a Japanese."
   —John Treacy

◆

"People don't realize that Mexicans, not Africans, are the dominant road runners today."
   —Salvador Garcia, after winning the 1991
   New York City Marathon

"Sometimes that guy [Garcia] talks too much. We Mexicans have come a long way, but we have yet to prove that we are faster than the Africans."

—**Jesus Herrera,** prior to 1992 Boston Marathon

◆

"This man, a lawyer by profession, is also a student of Aztec culture, and he told us the Mexican runner has something. . . we *remember* something from our long forgotten past. When we do take up running, we find it's a discipline that's familiar to us and that we recognize as something very good and very natural. This man said that my knowledge was inbred; he said when I go out training, I'm *remembering*. Ever since I began running, I've come up with those theories that later proved out."

—**Rudolfo Gomez,** 1984

◆

"The only wall Benoit ever hit was the outfield fence with a double in the gap at the Bowdoin alumni day soft-ball game."

—**Amby Burfoot,** on Joan Benoit Samuelson

◆

"Horace had taken second so many times I wondered why he didn't give up running."

> —**Mrs. Horace Ashenfelter Sr.,** on her son who (eventually) won the 1952 Olympic steeplechase

◆

"Pre was like Henry the Fifth. He didn't rule very long, but he left a big mark."

> —**Ken Kesey,** author of *One Flew Over the Cuckoo's Nest*, and Oregon track fan

◆

"I don't count the years. Men may steal my chickens, men may steal my sheep. But no man can steal my age."

> —**Miruts Yifter**

◆

"There are three things you don't bet against. They are taxes, death—and Alberto."

> —**Bill Squires,** 1981 (on Salazar)

◆

"The old lion is not dead yet!"

> —**Said Aouita,** after setting a indoor world record of 7:36.66 for 3000 meters in March, 1992

2. Nicknames

"The Flying Finn"	—Paavo Nurmi
"The Flying Wolf"	—Ville Ritola
"Gunder the Wonder"	—Gunder Hägg
"King of the Roads" or	
"Boston Billy"	—Bill Rodgers
"The Rookie"	—Alberto Salazar
"The Little Gazelle of Constantine"	
	—Hassiba Boulmerka
"The Prince of the Desert" or	
"The Black Knight" or	
"The Moroccan Express"	—Said Aouita
"Rambo"	—Francesco Panetta
"Pre" or "The Rube"	—Steve Prefontaine
"Tree" or "Deek"	—Rob de Castella
"Tarzan"	—Ellison Brown
"The Pride of Pawtucket"	—Les Pawson
"Bricklayer Bill"	—Bill Kennedy
	(Boston Marathon champ, 1917)
"The Gray Ghost"	—Norm Higgins
"Deerfoot"	—Lewis Bennett
"The Panther"	—Pat Porter

"Rat"	—Jeff Atkinson
"The Fabulous Frenchman"	—Gerard Cote
"Mr. DeMarathon"	—Clarence DeMar
"El Caballo" (the Horse)	—Alberto Juantorena
"The Kansas Cowboy"	—Wes Santee
"The Milwaukee Meteor"	—Archie Hahn
	(gold medals in three events at 1904 Olympics)
"Gentleman John"	—John Landy
"Fat"	—Ron Clarke
	(family nickname from his youth)
"The Buckeye Bullet"	—Jesse Owens
"King Carl"	—Carl Lewis
"The Chairman of the Boards" or	
"Steamin' Eamonn"	—Eamonn Coghlan
"Iron Man" or	
"Galloping Glenn"	—Glenn Cunningham
"Ox"	—Eino Oksanen
"Serious George"	—George Bonhag
"The Tiger Runner," or	
"Old Nassau" or "Bonny Bill"	—Bill Bonthron
"The Czech Choo Choo" or	
"Emil the Terrible"	—Emil Zatopek
"Juha the Cruel"	—Juha Väätäinen
"Yifter the Shifter"	—Miruts Yifter

"The Zen Kenyan"   —Douglas Wakiihuri

"The Eternal Second"   —Alain Mimoun
> (because he was second to Zatopek so many times—until the 1956 Olympic marathon)

"The Speedy Son of the Forest" or

"The Onondaga Wonder" or

"The Indian Iron Man" or

"The Streak of Bronze"   —Tom Longboat
> (Canadian Indian)

"The Jarrow Arrow"   —Steve Cram

"Big Bren"   —Brendan Foster

"Mr. Unpredictable"   —Pekka Vasala

"The Webbmaster"   —Alan Webb

Pain

There be some sports are painful, and their
labour
Delight in them sets off.
—**Shakespeare**, *The Tempest*

PAIN

One of the stories involving infamous Watergate tough guy G. Gordon Liddy has it that he, on occasion, would hold his hand in a candle flame to demonstrate his ability to withstand pain longer than the average human being. Liddy's flesh-in-flame display drew a variety of responses from softer souls, but someone once said, "Okay, so what's the trick?"

"The trick," Liddy reportedly replied, "is not minding."

Competitive runners often tightrope the red line between pure, unadulterated pain and something less severe, say, discomfort. Experienced distance runners are used to discomfort—a familiar training companion. In fact, we purposely venture out of our comfort zone in training—those sizzling speed sessions, killer hill work-outs, or even a several hour distance run—where the lactic acid flows freely. This "venturing out" toward the borders of pain is Nietschean in both quest and theory: "What does not destroy me makes me stronger"—or something like that.

Some people endure pain better than others. All things considered, the ability to withstand—or even deny—pain would seem to be a valuable ally for the long distance runner in search of significant improvement. In truth, it is probably a double-edged sword, since medical experts tell us that pain is the body's warning signal to back off, and that to ignore such schedules is to roll the dice with both body and mind.

At the peak of his career, Alberto Salazar was not the kind of man to heed the warnings of some academic study on the signals of pain and the possible downside of ignoring the same. Salazar could, in the words of speed-record test pilots, "push the edge of the envelope." Undoubtedly, Salazar's toughmindedness allowed him to win some close races at a world-class level in which men of less fortitude might have given up. But in the long run, that same ability may have damaged his health and short-ened his career. Even by the time the 1984 Olympic Games rolled around, Salazar—still in his mid-20s at the time—appeared to be on the downside of a career that had featured victories at the Boston ('82) and New York City marathons (1980-82). Comeback attempts proved to be unproductive—Salazar never recovered his world-beating form of the early 1980s.

"It was so frustrating because I wanted to run well,"

said Salazar in a 1994 interview with *Runner's World*, "but I was always sick and injured. In retrospect, I now know what was wrong and what caused my problems. I had three episodes of heatstroke [Falmouth '77, NCAAs '81 and Boston '82]. That, combined with all the years of hard training at such a high level without ever taking a break, damaged part of my brain. As a result, some of my bodily systems began to shut down."

Runners can die in competition—and not just out-of-shape plodders who enter marathons without physical exams where a hint of heart trouble might have been discovered. Heatstroke—especially in marathons—is a big concern; hence all the controversy about whether or not officials should have yanked Gabriele Andersen off the track when she staggered into the stadium at the L. A. Games in '84.

In the 1912 Olympic Games staged in Stockholm, twenty-one-year-old Francisco Lazaro was one of sixty-eight competitors in the marathon. A three-time national champion at the distance in Portugal, Lazaro was no novice. But nineteen miles into the race he collapsed with heatstroke and was rushed to a nearby hospital. Lazaro lay on the bed, feverish and unconscious—ironically, just blocks away from where a large crowd toasted and celebrated with South Africans Kenneth McArthur and Chris Gitsham who had won the gold and silver medals in the race. Lazaro died in his small room the next day. A bystander noted: "In his delirium, he seemed to still be struggling in the marathon."

"Suffering is the sole origin of consciousness."
> —**Dostoyevsky**

"It is horrible, yet fascinating, this struggle between a set purpose and an utterly exhausted frame."
> —**Sir Arthur Conan Doyle** after observing Italy's Dorando Pietri collapse three times in the last 100 meters of the 1908 Olympic Marathon

"It was impossible to leave him there, for it looked as if he might die in the very presence of the Queen."
> —**Official Olympic report** on why officials helped Pietri across the line

"It's at the borders of pain and suffering that the men are separated from the boys."
> —**Emil Zatopek**

◆

"Where am I?"
> —**Ron Clarke**'s first words upon regaining consciousness on the stadium infield at Mexico City

◆

"No pain, no gain."
> —**Athletic proverb**

◆

"No brain, no pain."
> —**Corollary to above**

◆

"No pain, no Spain."
> —**Maxim** popular with athletes prior to Barcelona Olympics

◆

"Few understand the mental agony through which an athlete must pass before he can give his maximum—and how rarely, if he is built such as I, he can give it."
> —**Sir Roger Bannister**

"High-performance sport is hell. You run intervals until your lactic acid rises and you faint. You think you are killing yourself. No weekends. No vacations. The sacrifice of living away from your family and friends."
 —**Hassiba Boulmerka**

◆

"Run like hell and get the agony over with."
 —**Clarence DeMar**

◆

"What counts in battle is what you do once the pain sets in."   —**John Short**, South African coach

"The fear of running a long race can come from the fact that you know it's going to be physically painful. And unless you are a masochist, nobody likes pain. And if you dwell on this, it can make you nervous."
 —**Ron Hill** on the marathon

◆

"Top results are reached only through pain. But eventually you like this pain. You'll find the more difficulties you have on the way, the more you will enjoy your success."
 —**Juha "the Cruel" Väätäinen**

"In the last fifty yards, my body had long since exhausted its energy but it went on running just the same."
   —Sir Roger Bannister

◆

"My body ached, I seemed to be suffocating, sweat blurred my vision."
   —Derek Ibbotson, 1957, on his 3:57.2

◆

"Near the end of the race I felt like I was breathing fire. I needed oxygen and my head felt like it was in a vice."
   —Lasse Viren concerning hot conditions in the
   Moscow 10,000, where he placed 5th

◆

"It was a new kind of agony for me. I had never run myself into such a state. My head was exploding, my stomach ripping, and even the tips of my fingertips ached. The only thing I could think was, 'If I live, I will never run again!'"
   —Tom Courtney, on his Olympic 800 win, 1956

◆

"My effort was over and I collapsed almost unconscious, with an arm on either side of me. It was only then that real pain overtook me. I felt like an exploded flashlight with no will to live; I just went on existing in the most passive physical state without being unconscious."

—Sir Roger Bannister

◆

"My legs aching, my chest aching, my heart thumping and banging away, the only things to look forward to, the only things that kept me going, the drinks of water; but only when he offered them, I'd never ask for them, no matter how I felt, any more than I'd stop till the old bastard said I could stop. Except twice to be sick, while he just stood watching me while it all came heaving out, not saying anything; just standing, waiting for me to go on, while I thought *Christ I'll die, I'm going to die, my guts are coming out, I'll die.*"

—Ike Low, miler in *The Olympian*

◆

"To keep from decaying, to be a winner, the athlete must accept pain—not only accept it, but look for it, live with it, learn not to fear it."

—Dr. George Sheehan

◆

"Muscle has been grinding, sinew against bone—that's not like golf."

> —**Bill Rodgers** on the possible future of a
> "masters running circuit"

◆

"It is not gymnastics or ice skating, you know."

> —**Emil Zatopek**, when questioned about his
> agonized expression while racing

◆

"Out of the silver heat mirage he ran. The sky burned, and under him the paving was a black mirror reflecting sun-fire. Sweat sprayed his skin with each footstrike, so that he ran in a hot mist of his own creation. With each slap on the softened asphalt, his soles absorbed heat that rose through his arches and ankles and the stems of his shins. It was a carnival of pain, but he loved each stride because running distilled him to his essence and the heat hastened this distillation."

> —**James Tabor**, from "The Runner," a short story

◆

"He was hardly aware of the crowd despite the incredible din. He had discovered the one force that could shut out everything else in the world: pain. Pain was insistent and it was absolute. It fed upon itself, and it fed upon him. It had begun to devour him, organ by organ, cell by cell." —**Bruce Tuckman**, from his novel, *Long Road to Boston*

◆

"The blood was boiling into his eyes along with the tears, and under his heart were red-hot coals. Loose bird-shot filled his throat and the faces of the crowd floated by like painted faces in a dream."

—**George Harmon Coxe**, "See How They Run," a short story

◆

"Wasn't it Percy Cerruty who said, 'When you see pain, embrace it'? I always liked that statement

—**Thom Hunt,** world-class runner in the 1980s

◆

"When I walked off the track, I stood there for a moment and I thought of all the hard work I had done to get to the Olympics—and I saw roads, snow, thunder, ice. I consider myself a pretty tough person and they say tough people don't cry. But I went under the stadium to hide. And I cried."

> —**Todd Williams,** on dropping out with exhaustion from his 1996 Olympic 10,000m semi-final

◆

"You hear a lot of comments about, 'He makes it look easy,' or 'His face shows no effort. . . .' Come look at my face in January when I'm trail-running in Texas and I'm hurting like a dog. It's an ugly face. But I'd rather have the face then and feel good here. It's called sacrifice."

> —**Lance Armstrong,** cycling great, en route to his third consecutiveTour de France victory, 2001

◆

"At least in a race you have mile markers and know how long you have to go. Labor is like running as hard as you can without knowing where the finish line is."

> —**Lorraine Moller,** Olympic Marathon bronze medalist in 1992, new mom at age 44 in 2000, comparing childbirth to marathoning

The Olympics

"There are enough irksome and troublesome things in life; aren't things just as bad at the Olympic festival? Aren't you scorched there by the fierce heat? Aren't you crushed in the crowd? Isn't it difficult to freshen yourself up? Doesn't the rain soak you to the skin? Aren't you bothered by the noise, the din and other nuisances? But it seems to me that you are well able to bear and indeed gladly endure all this, when you think of the gripping spectacles that you will see."

—**Epictetus**, Dissertations, 1st-2nd century A.D.

THE OLYMPICS

The Olympic Games have meant both glory and contro-versy, almost from inception. In 776 B.C., the Greek poet Pindar wrote: "No contest than Olympia greater to sing . . . " But in 67 A.D., the Roman Emperor Nero fixed the chariot race so he could win and things didn't get better as time went on.

It took about three more centuries until the Games ended (not to be revived until some fifteen centuries later by the French Baron Pierre de Coubertin) and opinion of the time might have been best summed up by Menander, an Athenian playwright specializing in comedy. Menander described the Games as "Fair, market, acrobats, fun and thieves."

The Olympics are a dual proposition that has both the potential to inspire—or disgust. Zeus was the primary god of the Games for the founding Greeks, but perhaps Janus—the two-faced Roman god would have been more appropriate as the centuries went by.

For those in need of a modern day example, picture marathoners wilting in the late-day August heat and humidity of Atlanta. Any Olympic bureaucrat, politician or television fat cat who thinks that's a fabulous idea should have to run the course under three hours themselves—or be shot with a starting pistol, preferably one containing live bullets.

Even de Coubertin warned that the Games could be manipulated for either good or evil and could "set in motion the most noble passions or the most vile ones. [The Olympic Movement] can be chivalric or corrupt."

And so there are boycotts, money-driven decisions, athletes who cheat, even occasional incidents of terrorism. And yet, how can we conclude anything other than how Epictetus so fittingly describes it on the chapter page quotation that the "gripping spectacle" is worth whatever must be endured?

Where is the Olympic glory? It is where you should always look for glory—within the individual. It was with Viren in 1972, when he fell, got up, and raced back into the lead in the 10,000. It was with Mills in Tokyo, charging on the outside, thinking: "I can win . . . I can win . . . I can win!" It was with Benoit in Los Angeles, thinking: "When you leave this tunnel, your life will be changed forever."

And it is with those who died before their time. With

the Israeli athletes . . . With Ethiopia's Abebe Bikila . . . With Steve Prefontaine . . . With Belgium's Ivo Van Damme . . . With Portugal's Francisco Lazaro . . . With Poland's Bronislaw Malinowski . . . With New Zealand's Jack Lovelock.

Olympic athletes are not gods, but to the rest of us strivers they come quite close to our immortal ideals. The embody our hopes, dreams, and courage. They represent the pinnacle of human physical achievement.

" "

"The most important thing in the Olympic Games is not to win but to take part, just as the most important thing in life is not the triumph but the struggle."
  —**Baron de Coubertin**, founder of the modern
    Olympic Games, 1890

"I'd like to be in a position to win an Olympics so I could offer the next guy a dead heat. That's my ultimate ambition. If he didn't want to accept a tie I'd step aside and say: 'It's all yours' The press conference later would be a beauty. They'd say: 'Why did you do it?' and I'd reply 'Winning isn't everything you bastards!'"

—**Chris Wardlaw**, Australian marathoner

◆

"We all know that Luxembourg does not expect to win any gold medal at Helsinki. Even Monsieur Barthel will be no Olympic champion, but as you know, the important thing in the Olympic Games is not so much winning as taking part."

—A **German official** at a Luxembourg-Germany dinner prior to the 1952 games. Barthel won the 1500 meters

◆

"I once read where, after Jim [Ryun] lost in the Olympics, some old Olympic official said to him. 'You let your country down.' I would have liked to have hung him from the Olympic flagpole for saying something like that. How anybody like that could even get near the Olympics amazes me."

—**Marty Liquori**

◆

"The wreath or death!"

—A common oath of ancient Olympians

"No contest than Olympia greater to sing."
　　　—Pindar, 776 B.C.

◆

"Fair, market, acrobats, fun, and thieves."
　　　—Menander, Athenian comic playwright,
　　　　describing the Olympic Games in A.D. 394

◆

"Instead of having elimination heats for the athletes they should have them for the fans. That way you wouldn't have a bunch of clowns here simply because it's the place to be."
　　　—Ron Clarke, comment when people jeered
　　　　Khalid Skah upon accepting his gold medal at
　　　　the Barcelona Olympics

◆

"The guys I work with in the insurance office all sent me off by saying things like how they can't wait to see my gold medal. I appreciate their enthusiasm for me, but I don't want to spend the rest of my life going to cocktail parties being introduced as either, 'Rick Wohlhuter, the Olympic champion,' or, 'Rick Wohlhuter, the Olympic choke.' That's the thing about these Games. You're remembered for what you do here and nothing else. But I don't want to make the Olympics into something they're not—and they're not the pinnacle of your life. That's the only way you can look at it if you want to keep your sanity."

—Rick Wohlhuter

◆

"You know, fourth is the absolutely worst place to finish in the Olympics."

—Eamonn Coghlan, who finished fourth, twice

◆

"After all those dark days of the war, the bombing, the killing, the starvation, the revival of the Olympics was as if the sun had some out. . . . I went into the Olympic Village and suddenly there were no more frontiers, no more barriers. Just the people meeting together. It was wonderfully warm. Men and women who had just lost five years of life were back again."

—Emil Zatopek, on the London Olympics, 1948

◆

"It's time somebody took the bloody flag out of games little boys play. . . . Sports as an instrument of international policy is spitballs against a battleship."

—Jim Murray, *L. A. Times,* 1976

"They [Nigerian government officials] tell me to run right, I run right. They tell me to run left, I run left. They tell me to go home, I go home. There's nothing we can do. When the home government says to go home, you go home."

—Nigerian hurdler **Taiwo Ogunjobi** regarding the African boycott of 1976

◆

"It leaves a sour taste in my mouth anytime somebody mentions Jimmy Carter. . . .We got cheated out of an experience of a lifetime for nothing. I didn't see them [the White House] boycotting selling grain or computers to the Russians. No one else sacrificed a bit except the athletes."

—**Steve Scott**, 1986

◆

"THE ROAD TO MOSCOW ENDS HERE."

—**Gary Fanelli**'s t-shirt at the Olympic Trials, 1980

◆

"The athletes have to give up a little freedom, and the country has to give up two or three MX missiles."

—**Brooks Johnson**, coach, on the necessary sacrifices for Olympic success

"Some do well in other races, some run fast times, but they cannot do well in the ultimate, the Olympics. . . . The question is not why I run this way, but why so many others can not."

      —**Lasse Viren** on peaking

◆

"The Games are littered with people who had one good day and were never heard of or seen again."

      —**Sebastian Coe**, 1979

◆

"Emil, why don't you congratulate me? I am an Olympic champion. It was I who won."

      —**Alain Mimoun** to Zatopek after winning the
      Olympic Marathon in Melbourne

◆

"I had always imagined an Olympic champion was something more than a mere mortal, in fact, a god. Now I knew he was just a human being."

      —**Murray Halberg**, on winning his gold medal

◆

"If I didn't have Olympic champion luck I had other luck and silver medals. Remember, to be second behind Herb Elliott is like being an Olympic Champion."
　　—Michel Jazy

◆

"The idea behind the Olympics is winning, not going after a record or sensational time. So the 'ideal final' for me would be the weakest possible field—perhaps a grandmother or two and some other senior citizens. It's the gold medal that counts, and I want to go after it."
　　—John Walker

◆

"It is thrilling to win a Gold Medal. Second place counts for nothing! The records don't matter. It's the medals that really count."
　　—Gaston Roelants

◆

"It was the amateurs who built Noah's Ark, but it was the professionals who designed and built the Titanic."
　　—Sir Arthur Gold, former chair of the British
　　　　Olympic Association, commenting on
　　　　increasing professionalization of the Games

Medals and Money

"The devotion of the true amateur athlete is the same devotion that makes an artist starve in his garret rather than commercialize his work."

—**Avery Brundage**, IOC president from 1952 to 1972 (and also a millionaire)

MEDALS AND MONEY

Two short stories, one on medals and one on money. . . .
I think they are both true, but here in *The Quotable
Runner* it's fair to say that—in the event of a close race—
we would not let the facts out-lean a good story, quote,
quip or snippet at the wire.

The medal story goes something like this: Rod Dixon,
the dashing Kiwi with the Erroll Flynn mustache, naturally was elated with his bronze medal finish in the
Munich 1500 in 1972. At least, that is, until he arrived at
drug testing and officials demanded that he produce a
urine specimen. Pre-race nerves and attention to proper
hydration are guaranteed to push any runner's bladder
into high gear *before* the race. Afterward, however, is
another story.

Such was Dixon's plight at Munich. Time passed. He
drank copious amounts of liquid. Still no luck. Finally,
the New Zealander produced a trickle into the plastic
cup and appealed to the drug testing officials. Was this
enough? The German officials peered at the meager
amount hovering just below the ideal level of liquid
requested, their faces etched with the Teutonic proclivity

to adhere to proper procedure. Dixon, in turn, looked on pleadingly, anxious to leave and begin some well-earned celebration that undoubtedly would involve replenishing his fluids with some of Munich's world-famous beers.

Finally, one of the officials shrugged, relinquished a wry smile and said: "For the gold medal, no, but for the bronze medal, it will do."

Now, about money. Money, of course, can be a great motivator to any athlete and runners are no exception. Consider this well-documented story concerning Orlando Pizzolato's most memorable marathon win. During the 1984 New York City Marathon, held on October 28, the temperature rose to an unseasonable 79 degrees and—worse yet—the Big Apple was all but withering in 90 percent humidity. Pizzolato of Italy pushed to a sizable lead through Harlem, but at mile 22, he grabbed at his side and stopped. Given the stifling conditions and the accumulation of his own fatigue, it seemed almost an action of sanity.

But not to a certain New York City motorcycle cop, whose assignment for the day was to accompany the race leader. Every time the Italian stopped, the police officer, perched comfortably on his machine, was incredulous and yelled in a language that Pizzolato thoroughly understood: "*Cinquantamila dollari! Cinquantamila dollari!*" (Fifty thousand dollars! Fifty thousand dollars!) Pizzolato stopped several times more. He could not help it. And each time the cycle cop bellowed "*Cinquantamila dollari! Cinquantamila dollari!*" Pizzolato began to trot again, eventually winning—although in a heat-slowed shuffle of 2:14—his fifty thousand *dollari*.

" "

"We lived for a month on a diet of convenience store oatmeal-cream cookies. We were up at 9,000 feet in the high desert, really cold, and no money to buy coffee, and no electricity to make it, and no mugs even to drink it out of. . . . [Michael] came back from running all sweaty, and because there was no heat in the camper/trailer, his clothes would just freeze solid."

—**Laura Mykytok,** on training in Flagstaff,
    Arizona, just before she "broke through"
    on the roads

"If Pavarotti receives $600,000 a night to sing, tell me why can't an athlete like Bubka receive $50,000 when he breaks a world record? Artistically speaking, I adore Pavarotti, but the [financial] difference is enormous. Yet the talent is great in both men."

—**Dr. Primo Nebiolo**, president of the
International Amateur Athletic Federation

◆

"I feel that the government should make it possible for a real artist to train and perform. Athletes should have the same opportunities as other artists and performers do, to perfect themselves through scholarships and fellowships to become artists in their sports."

—**Mario Moniz Pereira**, coach of Carlos Lopes

◆

"Clubs, promoters, newspaper journalists, officials, even countries, can gain kudos and prestige, but when the athlete who helps produce all this accepts his share in augmented expenses he is deemed a professional and excluded. How utterly puerile and dishonest."

—**Percy Cerutty**

◆

"That weekend I won the cross-country [nationals], Joe Namath who was in the same college year but in Alabama, signed a $400,000-a-year contract with the New York Jets. It was the biggest contract ever negotiated at the time. My father said: 'You got zip—this little medal.' The winning was memorable, but the limitations of having won it were even more so."

—Kenny Moore

"The world-class runner trains a thousand hours a year. If he were to make $4000 a year from his racing, he, the great virtuoso of his sport, would be earning the salary of a temporary office worker."

—Manfred Steffny, German marathoner, 1978

"But of course things have changed now. We used to run just for the honor, for the glory, just to show people we could do it. The people run now because of the money involved, because of the contracts, because of the sponsors, etc. We always did it just for the honor, the honor of our country, the honor of our federation. This is what we were in it for."

—Gaston Roelants

"When I look to the future I am sometimes frightened to think of the economic sacrifices I have made. At thirty I retire from athletics as a married man with no job and no prospects. After ten years of struggle to make ends meet, what have I gained except the privilege of running with a Union Jack on my chest?"

> —**Gordon Pirie**, great British distance runner
> of the 1950s

◆

"Running is the world's greatest sport, with the best athletes. It requires so much physical and mental energy, a real commitment. . . . There's no reason why the top runners shouldn't make every bit as much as the best is other sports. I came up when the runner was exploited, when he couldn't receive an honest day's pay. I think I helped change things. Maybe I went too far in the other direction but I was one of the first in this sport to call himself a professional runner, and I'm proud of that."

> —**Bill Rodgers**

◆

"[Athletes] should be protected against advertising exploitation. . . . However, if the individual wants to become a pro, then jolly good luck to him!"

> —**Lord Killanin**, IOC president, 1974

"You will have people entering the sport who are professional advertising men, professional administrators, professional managers. It's going to be a big world and if the athletes aren't careful they are going to get swallowed up."
—Sebastian Coe

◆

"At present I still have to get permission to go to a race at which I might win $10,000 to $15,000, far more than I earn in a whole year with the RAF."
>**—Steve Jones**, corporal/technician in 1984 after winning the Chicago Marathon in a world record 2:08:05

◆

"My mother had complained that I never win the car."
>**—Juma Ikangaa**, after his record-setting win at the New York Marathon in 1989 won him a Mercedes-Benz

◆

"When runners win a big race these days, they get a car. When I won a big race, I got a ride."
—Ron Delany

◆

"One time my daughter asked if I'd come to school and show her class my gold and silver medals. So I did. And a few days later, I got this letter that began: 'Dear Mr. Shorter. . . . Thank you for showing us your gold and silver medals that you won in the Olympics. Next time I hope you get a bronze to complete the set.'"

—**Frank Shorter,** before the 1992 Olympic trials

◆

"Once my daughter asked if she could take my Olympic gold medal to school for "Show and Tell." I said that she could. Then I was curious about what she might say, so I showed up in her classroom that day and sat in the back. My daughter got up before the class and held up my medal and said: 'This is just like the medal Peggy Fleming won for ice skating.'"

—**Billy Mills**

◆

"It's the most boring subject in the world to have to keep talking about amateurism. Even to say the word leaves a sick taste in my mouth . . . nauseating."

—**Bill Rodgers**

◆

"I'm just like any other American. If I don't pay my electric bill, they turn off my lights. After college, our athletes are turned out to pasture. We have no Olympic program in this country. It's as simple as that. No sports medicine, no camps, no nothing. I'm not talking about subsidizing us. I'm just talking about a national plan. I want to see some interest from somebody. In the past, we've sat back and let our natural talent do it. Well, the rest of the world has caught up."

   —Steve Prefontaine, 1975

◆

"When you're at the starting line, the last thing you think about is money. When you're at the finish line, it's the first thing you think about."

   —Rod Dixon

◆

"What I get on the roads is someday going to be considered laughable by the top athletes."

   —Bill Rodgers, 1981

◆

"I've turned down many lucrative offers to run marathons because I want my career to be as good as it can be. . . . I would rather not race many times for just money; I would rather win little bits of metal at the end of a colored ribbon."

> —**Charles Spedding**, 1984 Olympic bronze medalist

◆

"Medals are nice, but they are only symbols."

> —**Emil Zatopek** (He gave his Helsinki 10,000 gold to WR setter Ron Clarke of Australia.)

◆

"A medal is an insult to an athlete! His achievement is sufficient in itself."

> —Coach **Sam Dee**, fictional coach in Brian Glanville's *The Olympian*

◆

"The medals have no sentimental value for me. What does it matter whether they are with me or someone else?" —**Lasse Viren**, 1994, on why he put his four Olympic gold medals up for sale

◆

"Besides, a medal is only a thing, an object. The race, the achievement, is what's most important. I think the medal is still on the floor of my car—among the diapers."

—**Joan Nesbit,** after skipping the World Indoor
3000 meter awards ceremony to return home
to her two-year-old daughter, Sarah Jane

◆

"The best way to answer that is, if I could play golf and make money, I'd be playing golf and making money. I'd be able to support my family. I don't think the sacrifice is ever going to be worth it when you've got a family."

—**Greg Fredricks,** former U.S. recordholder for
10,000m, when asked: "Is running worth it?"

◆

"It's not like being a professional in a team sport where you get paid whether you win or lose. If I don't race, I don't make money. If I get hurt, it's an emotional, physical and financial disaster."

—**Jon Sinclair**

◆

"The problem is most athletes give up a safe job or a family way of life and at the end all they're left with is a bunch of medals. Unfortunately medals don't pay for mortgages."
   —**John Walker**

◆

"You can't eat trophies."
   —**Ellison "Tarzan" Brown**

◆

"I was given three hundred crowns after a race, 'for your splendid running' the man told me. I couldn't believe that I was given money for something I enjoyed so much. But soon it became a habit for someone to offer me money before a race. At first I didn't know what to say and I paused. That made the organizer think I wasn't satisfied—so he raised his offer. After a few times, I kept my mouth shut. Anyway, the stadia were full for my sake, weren't they? After all, I never *asked* for money; they *offered* it. So I took it. Would I have run if I hadn't been offered money? Of course not."
   —**Gunder Hägg**

◆

"At the start of the 1947 track season I was just besieged with invitations to run for the AAA in various matches, but hardly had the season opened when I got badly blistered feet through wearing poorly made spikes. At this time, I was still not in a position to buy a really expensive hand-made pair—even though I was the national six mile champion."

> **—Jim Peters**

◆

"I remember winning a race at Salem (Mass.), and they gave me a pair of shoes—leather, business-type shoes for a professional to wear to a job. I took them and walked away, and an old geezer came up and said, 'You know you can't accept those shoes, don't you? You'll jeopardize your opportunity to run in the Pan American Games.' The shoes were worth more than $35, and that was the limit then. More than $35, and you were a professional."

> **—John J. "Young John" Kelley,** Boston
> Marathon champ in 1957

◆

"Hey, with this the money's guaranteed!"

> **—Ed Eyestone,** on why he choose to comment
> for TV at the 1994 Bloomsday race instead of
> running

"I ran a race in Montreal once and won a refrigerator. It was the craziest race I've ever run. Twenty-six miles in a ballpark; 118 times around the field! There was a band playing and fire broke out in the right field bleachers. The guy who organized it lost his shirt because he rented the ballpark. Montreal had a farm team. They were on the road and I got to use Jackie Robinson's locker. I beat Cote by a lap or so and won the refrigerator. Tarzan Brown won a refrigerator once down in Bridgeport, Connecticut, but he lived out in the woods and had no electricity, so he sold it."

—John A. "Old John" Kelley

◆

"There's a small marathon over in Barcelona in the middle of August, so I'm going to run there, but there's no prize money, so I'm doing it just for the fun."

—John Treacy, prior to '92 Olympic Games

◆

"A runner must run with dreams in his heart, not money in his pocket."

—Emil Zatopek

◆

"I won twenty thousand dollars at the Twin Cities Marathon. My mom called to ask: 'How'd you do? . . . Did you win a prize?' 'Yeah mom, I got a medal.' 'Did you win any money?' 'Yeah, I won $20,000.' 'Now good, you can stop running. You've made enough money.' But I don't do it for the money. The minute you start focusing on the money, you lose sight of what you got into the sport for in the first place."

—**Kim Pawelek,** seventh place finisher in the 2000 U.S. Olympic Marathon Trials

◆

"There's a lot of pressure to keep my record sparkling—no silvers or bronzes."

—**Michael Johnson,** Olympic sprint great

◆

"If I had to choose between a gold medal and a happy family life, I'd take the good family life every time."

—**Ron Clarke,** Australian distance great

The Finish Line:
Retirement

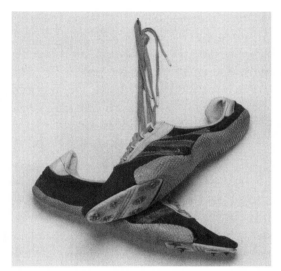

Then marvel not, thou great and complete man,
That all the Greeks begin to worship Ajax;
Since things in motion sooner catch the eye
Than what not stirs.

—Shakespeare, *Troilus and Cressida*

THE FINISH LINE
(Retirement)

Sometime after his two Olympic appearances, his training often interrupted by various injuries and professional demands on his time, Frank Shorter ran a race in Seattle. He finished somewhere out of the top twenty and was in the process of vacating the premises, when a mid-packer runner—wide-eyed with enthusiastic discovery—declared: "Hey, aren't you Frank Shorter?"

To which Shorter wryly replied: "No . . . But I used to be."

David Moorcroft, an Englishman, was at the top of his form in 1982 when he set a world record for 5000 meters. But by the middle of the decade—slowed by the usual wear and tear of running at a world class level—Moorcroft was struggling. One time during this difficult period, Moorcroft was laboring near the back of the pack in a cross-country race—whereupon his young son, perhaps 5 or 6 at the time, turned to Moorcroft's wife and, in a conspiratory whisper, said: "Shall we pretend that we don't know him, Mummy?"

Athletes, privileged lot that they are, even get to die

twice—once like everybody else, but first when they experience the end of their competitive careers. This is, of course, a significant part of A. E. Housman's famous poem "To An Athlete Dying Young":

> Now you will not swell the rout
> Of lads who wore their honor out,
> Runners whom renown outran
> And the name died before the man.

Wolfgang Goethe surely couldn't have had running in mind when he wrote this verse in "The Holy Longing," but viewed in the context of an Olympic runner's beautiful, if usually brief, presence on the world scene, it speaks to something in me:

> Distance does not make you falter
> now, arriving in magic, flying—
> and, finally, insane for the light,
> you are the butterfly and you are gone.

And in *The Olympian*, Brian Glanville's excellent novel about a British working class lad who becomes a world-class miler, similar images and philosophies are reflected. The book's cynical/intellectual sprinter Alan Bell muses:

> It's a sin and a shame that people like that can't spend their whole lives running. After all, it keeps them happy, they do no harm, they bring pleasure to people who watch them or support them. *Another glorious gold for Britain!* God, what a pity people aren't like insects; how sad they should outlive their function. They should be like butterflies: beautiful, flying about for their short span, then expiring, no anticlimax. A runner should live till his legs give out, a singer while she still has a voice, a film star till she's lost her looks. It would be so much kinder.

Great runners burst onto the scene, shatter world records, win gold medals, bring thousands in the stadium to their feet, and then, finally, inevitably, they disappear, as mere mortals must. There are framed pictures (sometimes, even statues), medals in bank vaults, or forgotten in the bottom of some cluttered desk drawer; and even the memories of such greatness can seem so elusive. Such is the transitory nature of success.

In the later years of his life, Jack Lovelock of New Zealand—the middle distance star of the 1930s—once said to his wife: "I don't know why I did it . . . All that running round and round a track."

" "

"Every runner is just one hamstring injury away from oblivion."
   —Steve Jones

◆

"I've strained my body to the bounds of endurance and running had become a nightmare."
   —Herb Elliott, upon his retirement at age 22

◆

"Time to hang up the spikes."
   —Athletic proverb

◆

"I feel like a boxer who looks great in the gym but as soon as he enters the ring gets knocked out. But then this is no longer life or death for me."

> —**Sebastian Coe**, retiring after a sixth-place finish in the Commonwealth Games 800 in 1990

"I have retired from the sport. I feel more like being with my family than hassling with meet directors."

> —**Howell Michael**, miler, 1975

"I compare it to a kid having a big jar of candy. At the beginning, you're stuffing your face with candy. Then, when you have only about a half-dozen pieces left, you start to savor them. You treat every race like it's special."

> —**Marcus O'Sullivan**, age 33, on nearing the end of his racing career

"We're conditioned to think that great athletes should stop competing when they're no longer great. But if you enjoy running as much as I do, what's wrong with continuing to do it even if you are no longer one of the best?"

> —**Steve Scott**, 1995, on his comeback after testicular cancer

"J. E. Lovelock may never run again because of a recent operation on the cartilage of his knee."

> —**Newspaper report** on Jack Lovelock, who then went on to win the 1936 Olympic 1500

◆

"You can regard your athletic career as finished."

> —**Doctor** to Gunder Hägg, age 20, after Hägg developed double pneumonia. The very next year he broke Jack Lovelock's WR for 1500

◆

"I never retired. . . . I just did other things."

> —**Edwin Moses** contemplating a comeback prior to the 1992 U.S. Olympic Trials

◆

"I can make a comeback if George Foreman can. He's eleven years older than I am, and none of my rivals is trying to punch me."

> —**Said Aouita**, age 35, in 1995

◆

"Comebacks, like political careers, very rarely end happily."

> —**Sebastian Coe**, 1995, on Aouita's attempt to return to world-class status

"Why am I still running? Well, I know myself: For 15 years, while I have not been a workaholic, I have been a runaholic. Some people can't live without booze; it looks like I can't live without running."

  —**Lasse Viren**, 1982, contemplating a comeback

"There is no finish line."

  —**Nike** advertising slogan

"The day I retire is the day they drop me into the fire or bury me."

  —**Ron Hill**

"Put away your spikes for good. The same Holland that demanded successes of you wants to keep the best memory. Render the sport this last service."

  —**A newspaper**'s "An appeal to Fanny" for Fanny
   Blankers-Koen's retirement after the Olympics

"The older I get the more the good times escape me."

  —**Ben Jipcho**

"Quit? Retire? Hell, no. Next year I'm really gonna train." —**Marty Liquori,** 1977

◆

"Today, I definitely qualify as a jogger. I realized that recently when I saw a beautiful golf course and my immediate thought was how great it would be to play on it, not run on it."

> —**Jon Anderson,** 1973 Boston Marathon winner, speaking in 1991

◆

"She'll come in handy when I need knee replacements."
> —**Keith Brantly** on his marriage to Pier Boutin, M. D., an orthopedic surgeon

◆

"Whenever you win a big race, there's always a letdown. And actually, the race has diminished in importance right after you've won it. It's gone. . . Once you start dwelling on it, I think it's time to retire. You know, you're over a beer in the bar telling everybody what a great runner you used to be."

> —**Frank Shorter,** after Munich, before Montreal

◆

"If you make one mistake, it can result in vasectomy."
  —**John Rowland**, Olympic medalist,
    on the steeplechase

◆

"Arne may not agree with me, but our best days are over. We have taken so much out of ourselves, and out of each other." —**Gunder Hägg**, 1945, when an up-and-coming
    young Swede, Lennart Strand, beat both Hägg
    Arne Andersson

◆

"Once a man was born to run perfectly. All other instances are for the convenience of others."
  —**Henry Rono**, disillusioned and contemplating
    retirement in 1986

◆

Victories and Defeats

"It eluded us then, but that's no matter. Tomorrow we will run faster . . . Stretch out our arms farther—And one fine morning . . ."
—**F. Scott Fitzgerald,** *The Great Gatsby*

VICTORIES AND DEFEATS

In *Thirty Phone Booths To Boston*, author Don Kardong relates a story of being in a taxi cab with Frank Shorter after running a road race in Charleston, West Virginia. Kardong could not resist telling the cabbie that he was transporting the famous runner. It took Kardong a few minutes, and some reluctant acknowledgement from Shorter himself, to convince the driver that one of his passengers was, indeed, the two-time Olympic marathon medalist.

Finally the cabbie, staring in the rear-view mirror, said: "You're really Frank Shorter, eh? . . . What happened to you at Montreal?"

Sport is not life and death, and yet there are winners and there are losers, victors and victims. And, yes, the occasional villain (unless we're including athletic bureaucrats, in which case there are enough villains to launch a Batman flick). But even the Olympians, as Halberg concluded, are, after all, just ordinary men and women. And being such, subject to the irresistible lure of mortal aspirations—and, therefore, of course, the entire array of corresponding human failings.

One of the shortest quotes in this book—a mere few words—is the translated suicide note of Japanese marathoner Kokichi Tsuburaya, the bronze medal winner at the 1964 Olympic Games in Tokyo. Although the gold and world record both fell easily to Ethiopia's Abebe Bikila's 2:12:11.2, Tsuburaya and Great Britain's Basil Heatley dueled for the silver. Tsuburaya entered the stadium ahead of the Englishman, holding second by about ten meters. But Heatley "stuck him" coming off the last turn—despite the encouragement of the partisan crowd of 75,000. Heatley clocked 2:16:19.2 for the silver, and Tsuburaya finished less than four seconds behind him. Tsuburaya's bronze represented the first medal won by Japan in track and field since 1936 and he was honored as a national hero.

But along with the recognition came pressure to perform; to reach for even greater heights four years distant at Mexico City. A member of the Japanese military defense force, Tsuburaya was ordered to break off a relationship with his girl friend and commence immediate training for the 1968 Olympic Games. Depressed over a series of injuries and subsequent weeks of hospitalization in 1967, Tsuburaya took his own life on January 9, 1968.

He left only this solitary phrase on a scrap of paper: "Cannot Run Anymore."

There have been several "blind" polls distributed among athletes, the gist of the questionnaire being this: If you could take a magic pill that would make you an Olympic champion in your event, but results in death several years later, would you do it? Those who have conducted these polls say that more than half of those who answer say that they *would* take the magic pill.

I once heard Kip Keino, the great Kenyan runner and two-time Olympic gold medalist, speak to hundreds of the nation's best high school track and field athletes at a meet near Chicago. One of Keino's most urgent messages was to turn away from performance-enhancing drugs. "When you are on the victory stand," said Keino, "you must be able to ask yourself: 'Did I win this medal?'"

I was in another country once and spent time there with a former world-class runner who had once tested positive for banned substances. The athlete had been a national hero in his country (as comparatively big, shall we say, as Pete Rose before his gambling debacle) prior to his fall from grace. Maybe I was surprised to find him to be a good guy and a great host. (What had I expected?

Some fire-breathing devil?). But sometimes when you looked at him, alone with himself, he seemed, maybe, to be one of the saddest people on the face of the earth.

" "

"The athlete is another painter, another composer, another poet where the famous paintings, the sublime music or the verses are replaced by world records. Athletics and running become a part of the story and tradition of the whole country in the future."
   —Gunder Hägg

◆

"A race is a work of art that people can look at and be affected in as many ways as they're capable of understanding."
   —Steve Prefontaine

◆

"If I am beaten the next time I run, I do not mind. If you have a salad that is all one thing, all lettuce, it is not good. It has no flavor. So victory, always, would be flat. You must mix it with defeat to gain the flavor."

—**Gerard Cote**, four-time Boston Marathon champion in the 1940s

◆

"There is nothing like standing on the start line of the 1500-meters. It always will be the blue ribbon event. It is the last day. The stadium is full. Everybody is watching. You feel like a gladiator. I'm Spartacus."

—**Peter Elliott**, 1500m silver medalist at Seoul

◆

"It came like electricity, it came from every fibre, from his fingertips to his toes. It came as broad waters come through a gorge. He called on it all."

—**Norman Harris**, description of Jack Lovelock's finishing kick to win the 1936 Olympic 1500

◆

"If I faltered, there would be no arms to hold me and the world would be a cold and forbidding place."

—**Sir Roger Bannister**

"It is simply that we can all be good boys and wear our letter sweaters around and get our little degrees and find some nice girl to settle, you know, *down* with . . . take up what a friend of ours calls the hearty challenges of lawn care . . . Or we can blaze! Become legends in our own time, strike fear in the heart of mediocre talent everywhere! We can scald dogs, put records out of reach! Make the stands gasp as we blow into an unearthly kick from three hundred yards out! We can become God's own messengers delivering the dreaded scrolls! We can race black Satan himself till he wheezes fiery cinders down the back straightaway. . . . They'll speak our names in hushed tones, 'those guys are animals' they'll say! We can lay it on the line, bust a gut, show them a clean pair of heels. We can sprint the turn on a spring breeze and feel the winter leave our feet! We can, by God, let our demons loose and *just wail on*!"

—**Quentin Cassidy**, fictional miler in
John Parker's *Once A Runner*

◆

"My life is a gift to me from my Creator. What I do with my life is my gift back to the Creator."

—**Billy Mills**

"Sport is not about being wrapped up in cotton wool. Sport is about adapting to the unexpected and being able to modify plans at the last minute. Sport, like all life, is about taking risks."

—Sir Roger Bannister

◆

"Once you leave this tunnel your life will be changed forever."

> **—Joan Benoit's** thoughts prior to entering the Olympic Stadium in L.A. en route to winning the first-ever Olympic Marathon for women

◆

"The events in my home town of Nelson were unbelievable. About 23,000 people turned up at the airport to welcome me home. I was carried shoulder-high up the main street with everyone wildly cheering. It was incredible that here I was being honored with a civic reception for winning a bronze medal. If I'd won gold they probably would have given me the keys to the city."

—Rod Dixon, after Munich

◆

"I vividly remember winning my first national cross-country championship in 1967. . . . I'd tried and tried to win this title for years, and although I'd been close, never cracked it. It was so exciting that it was impossible to sleep afterward. The next day on the plane back to Portland the stewardess was an old high school friend. She knew I'd won and put in first class with champagne and then placed an embarrassing announcement over the speaker system. Eugene airport was closed so I had to bus it from Portland. It was full of old reprobates and drunks. I was sitting next to this snoring drunk and on pulling into Eugene there was a reader board on a bank, the ones that give the news in lights, and my name was up there. I was about ready to elbow this sleeping guy and say: 'Look, it's me' and then I thought: 'What am I doing—nobody cares.' It's just personal satisfaction."

—**Kenny Moore**

◆

"If everybody could get in on this [running] on a world scale, it would really be hard for people to go to war."

—**Ron Dawes**, at the 1992 U.S. Marathon Trials

◆

"Unless you're an athlete you can't understand it. Joe Public can't understand it. All they see is you racing in Oslo, Spain etc. and there's all this talk about money. They don't see the other side of it: being really depressed and having to go to the physiotherapist twice a day, thinking your career is over. Or walking backwards down stairs because the Achilles is so tight."

—Peter Elliott

"You can't climb up to the second floor without a ladder. . . . When you set your aim too high and don't fulfill it, then your enthusiasm turns to bitterness. Try for a goal that's reasonable, and then gradually raise it."

—Emil Zatopek

"There are people who have no bodies, only heads. And many athletes have no heads, only bodies. A champion is a man who has trained his body *and* his mind, who has learned to conquer pain for his own purposes. A great athlete is at peace with himself and at peace with the world; he has fulfilled himself. He envies nobody. Wars are caused by people who have not fulfilled themselves."

—Coach **Sam Dee** in *The Olympian*

"I have to give up so many things, make so many personal sacrifices to perform at my level, that I cannot even contemplate losing."

—**Sebastian Coe**

◆

"I've given up the ten most productive years of my life to running, but look what I've gained. There's no way I can describe the incredible feeling of winning the Peachtree Road Race [1982] and hearing thousands and thousands of people calling my name. The sheer joy of it and the fantastic rush of winning a race like that are experiences few people will ever know."

—**Jon Sinclair**

◆

"Who are you? Who are you?"

—**Japanese official** to Billy Mills after he won the 10,000 in Tokyo

◆

"In the moment of victory I did not realize that the inner force, which had been driving me to my ultimate goal, died when I became the world's fastest miler."

—**Derek Ibbotson,** on his world record in 1957

"It was important for me to win this for Soh Kee-Chung, the hero of 1936. It was also for my mother who during the entire race was at the temple praying that I would win the gold for Korea."

—**Hwang Young-Jo,** South Korea,
1992 Olympic Marathon champ

◆

"I will always be the guy with the hat. The hat is more memorable than I am. It actually beat me into the Track and Field Hall of Fame by three years. Thinking back to Munich, I could take the high ground and say the 800 worked out just like I wanted, but in reality it was close to a disaster for me. I thought I could win the race, but I was so far behind right from the gun that it shook my confidence. As it turned out, I was able to maintain the same pace while everybody else faded badly at the end."

—**Dave Wottle**

◆

"It is very disappointing to lose in the last stride by the length of your nose."

—**Yevgeny Arzhanov,** Soviet 800 runner, "nosed"
by Dave Wottle in the 1972 Olympics

◆

"It's all fun—until you [expletive deleted] lose!"
   —Dave Bedford

◆

"It is interesting to contrast the reaction of the French public with that of Australians after the Tokyo Olympics. Michel [Jazy] had announced that he was considering retirement. When he returned home he was met at Orly Airport by a reported 6,000 well-wishers, and at his home 2,000 letters awaited him, most of them pleading with him to continue running. There was certainly no crowd at Melbourne Airport welcoming me (not that I expected one), nor any letters. The only comment I can remember was from a typically blunt Aussie: 'Why don't you give it away, sport?' Surely there are no people who can match Australians in their readiness to knock their own sportsmen."
   —Ron Clarke

◆

"Did you make a mental apology to Gordon Pirie yesterday? You were probably just one of thousands if you did, just one of those who called him a big-head, a windbag, a good distance runner who would never be a great one."
   —John Fairgrieve, British journalist, writing after
      Pirie beat Zatopek in 1955

"It's been upsetting that people have seen my attitude not as recklessness but weakness. The Australian behavior toward losers is far from healthy. If youngsters are taught that losing is a disgrace, and if they're not sure they can win, they will be reluctant to even try. And not trying is the real disgrace."

> **—Ron Clarke**

"It is probably rather good for one to take an occasional drubbing and, though I would naturally have preferred to win, I did not in the least begrudge Luigi [Becalli] his win. He is a delightful opponent. Two wins to him, the third is mine!"

> **—Jack Lovelock**, training diary

"Just as I always dreamed in secret. I raised my arms, I smiled and I crossed the finish line."

> **—Josy Barthel** of Luxembourg describing his
> 1952 1500 win

"I would rather have won this race than be President of the United States."

> —**Thomas Hicks** on his 3:28:53 marathon win in
> St. Louis in 1904

◆

"The highlight of my career was a string of road race victories that I don't think anybody will be able to match, but it was also my downfall. I raced two or three times a month, 12 months a year. I was on a roll and nobody beat me. . . . Being able to race every week and win was like a drug to me. I had to constantly feed that need."

> —**Herb Lindsay**, U.S. road racer, virtually
> unbeatable from 1979 to 1981

◆

"Great is the victory, but the friendship of all is greater."

> —**Emil Zatopek**

◆

"I think that's what it's all about—friendships of sport. If you're going to be an arsehole to others during your running career then you're not going to have many friends when you retire."

> —**Rod Dixon**

"It should have been the best feeling in the world when I caught him, but it wasn't. I didn't want to do this to Lucketz [Swartbooi] because he's such a nice man and had been passed like this in the last kilometer of his last three marathons. I almost hesitated before I got to him, but then I thought, he's 27 years old and will have many more opportunities. I had to pass him; this was *my* opportunity!"

—**Mark Plaatjes** on winning the 1993 World
Championship Marathon in Stuttgart

◆

"God's been good to me. I've caught a few bad breaks along the way, but God likes me. And I like Him, too. Time marches on and here I am way up in my 80s. Jeepers. I want to run till I'm 100. I'll never stop. People ask me about my philosophy of life all the time. I just put one foot in front of the other and keep going."

—**John A. "Old John" Kelley,** from
Young at Heart

◆

"We run, not because we think it is doing us good, but because we enjoy it and cannot help ourselves. . . . The more restricted our society and work become, the more necessary it will be to find some outlet for this craving for freedom. No one can say, 'You must not run faster than this, or jump higher than that.' The human spirit is indomitable."

—Sir Roger Bannister

◆

"You don't run against a bloody stopwatch, do you hear? A runner runs against himself, against the best that's in him. Not against a dead thing of wheels and pulleys. That's the way to be great, running against yourself. Against all the rotten mess in the world. Against God, if you're good enough."

—Bill Persons, fictional coach in Hugh
Atkinson's *The Games*

◆

"Ignore, then, whether you are tall and thin or short and stocky—whether they laughed at you at home (where they are often unkind) or at school (where they *are* mostly blind, anyway). Indeed—to hell with the lot of them if you 'feel' you can do it."

—Percy Cerutty

"Have a dream, make a plan, go for it. You'll get there, I promise."

        —**Zoe Koplowitz,** Achilles Track Club member
        with multiple sclerosis, who required 24 hours
        on crutches but finished the 1993 New York
        City Marathon.

◆

WHO'S WHO
in *The Quotable Runner*

ANDERSSON, Arne—Gunder Hägg's friend, countryman and rival, Andersson set world records for the mile (4:01.6 in 1944) and 1500 meters (3:44.9 in 1943). 126, 193, 270

AOUITA, Said—The dominant middle-distance runner of the 1980s, Aouita won the 5000-meter gold in Los Angeles. He also set world records at 1500, 2000, 3000 and 5000 meters. 116, 219, 220, 267

ARMSTRONG, Lance—American cycling great. Winner of the Tour de France in 1999, 2000, 2001 after beating cancer. 234

AUDAIN, Anne—New Zealand standout who won most of the major races on the American road racing scene in the early 1980s. She also set a world record for 5000 meters on the track and won a Commonwealth Games gold in the 3000. 23

BANNISTER, Roger—Although he failed to medal in the 1952 Olympic Games, Englishman Roger Bannister made history when he ran the first sub-4 minute mile, a 3:59.4 on May 6, 1954 at Oxford's Iffley Road track. Bannister also won the so-called "Mile of the Century" in his Empire Games showdown with Australia's John Landy, by less than a second in 3:58.8. Bannister became a doctor, was knighted, and headed Great Britain's "Sport For All" fitness movement. 24, 33, 53, 56, 100, 113, 134, 161, 189, 190, 192-5, 211, 215, 228, 230-1, 276, 278, 287.

BARRIOS, Arturo—Mexican-born runner, now a U.S. citizen. Barrios once held the world record for 10,000 meters (27:08.23 in 1989). 82

BARBER, Tiki—New York Giants football player. 157

BAYI, Filbert—Tanzanian runner, Bayi set world records for the 1500 (3:32.2) and the mile (3:51.0), plus won the silver medal in the 1980 Olympic steeplechase behind Poland's Bronislaw Malinowski. 82

BEDFORD, David—Colorful English runner, known for high mileage training schedules, Bedford once set a world record for 10,000 meters. 14, 81, 97, 283

BIKILA, Abebe—Ethiopian great who won the Olympic marathons in both Rome (2:15:16.2, barefoot!) and Tokyo (2:12:11.2) in world record times. Bikila was paralyzed in a car crash in 1969 and died in 1973 of a brain hemorrhage. 207, 216, 238, 273

BORDIN, Gelindo—Bordin came from behind to win the Seoul Olympic Marathon in 2:10:32. He also won the 1990 Boston Marathon. 180, 182, 207

BOWERMAN, Bill—Former coach at the University of Oregon where he developed the Ducks into a noted distance power, Bowerman was credited for the "hard/easy" day format of distance training and helping to ignite recreational running in America. 46, 51, 53, 55, 59-62, 85, 91, 98, 163

BRACE, Steve—Winner of the 1991 Berlin Marathon. 25

BRANTLY, Keith—U.S. road racer and marathon runner. 84, 269

CACHO, Fermin—Barcelona 1500m gold medalist. 23

CARROLL, Noel—Collegiate standout at Villanova, Irish-native Carroll coaches and writes on the sport for the *Irish Runner* magazine. 27

CERUTTY, Percy Wells—The late Australian coach of Herb Elliott, Albie Thomas and other great runners from Down Under in the 1950s and 1960s. Regarded by many as an eccentric, Cerutty was infamous for his "killer" hill sessions in the steep sand dunes of his training camp at Portsea. 21, 47, 50-1, 54, 57, 92, 151, 153, 202, 249, 287

CIERPINSKI, Waldemar—East Germany's Cierpinski won the Olympic Marathon in Montreal (1976) and Moscow (1980)—equaling Bikila's feat. 203

CLARKE, Ron—Great Australian distance runner of the 1960s, Clarke set a number of world records, including 5000 (13:16.6) and 10,000 meter (27:39.4) marks—both still Australian records 30 years after he ran them. Clarke was favored to win the Tokyo 10,000 (won by Billy Mills), but had to settle for a bronze. 5, 25-6, 38, 54, 94, 108, 114, 211, 221, 228, 240, 255, 260, 283, 284

CLAYTON, Derek—Australian runner who was the first man to run under 2:09 in the marathon. He placed 7th in the Mexico City Olympic Marathon.82, 135, 202, 213

COE, Sebastian—Voted the "Runner of the Quarter Century" by *Runner's World* magazine, Great Britain's Coe set world records for 800, 1000 and 1500 meters, as well as the mile. Coe was the only man to repeat as gold medalist in the 1500 (1980 and 1984). Seb was coached by his father, Peter Coe (p. 57). 90, 92, 127, 135, 192, 203, 207, 211, 243, 252, 266-7, 281

COGHLAN, Eamonn—Former Villanova great from Ireland, Coghlan won the 1983 world championship 5000 meters in Helsinki—some consolation for a pair of fourths in Olympic competition. In 1983, the "Chairman of the Boards" blazed a world-record 3:49.78 indoor mile at the Meadowlands in New Jersey. On February 20, 1994, at Harvard University's indoor track, the 41-year-old Coghlan ran 3:58.15—the first sub-4 minute mile ever by a master (40-years or over). 25, 152, 195, 216, 221, 241

COOPER, Ken, M.D.—Renowned exercise physiologist. 32

CORBITT, Ted—Marathoner and ultra-marathoner, Corbitt competed in the 1952 Olympic Marathon for the U.S. 85, 153, 182

COURTNEY, Thomas—Won the 1956 800 meters at Melbourne by one second over Great Britain's Derek Johnson in an Olympic record time of 1:47.7. Courtney's win gave the U.S.A. four straight Olympic victories in the 2-lap event. 106, 121, 230

CRAM, Steve—Silver medalist in the 1984 Olympic 1500, behind Sebastian Coe. Cram set three world records in twenty days in 1985: the 1500m (3:29.67); the mile (3:46.31); and the 2000m (4:51.39). 127, 132, 211, 222

De CASTELLA, Rob—Australian marathoner who won the gold medal in the 1983 World Championship race. He also won Japan's Fukuoka race and the Boston Marathon. 81, 86, 145, 151, 176, 181, 220

DANIELS, Jack—Former research physiologist for Nike's Athletics West teams, now coaching at the State University of New York. 58, 95-6, 206

DECKER, Mary—American middle-distance star. 169

DELANY, Ron—The 1956 Olympic champ at 1500 meters, Delany was one of the first great Irish middle distance runners to run for Jumbo Elliott at Villanova. 121, 216, 252

DELLINGER, Bill—Coach at the University of Oregon and of Alberto Salazar, Dellinger placed third in the 1964 Olympic 5000 meters. 86, 212

DEMAR, Clarence—Won the Boston Marathon seven times (1911, 1922, 1923, 1924, 1927, 1928 and 1930). He also competed on three U.S. Olympic Marathon teams, although he failed to win a medal. 24, 70, 221, 229

DIXON, Rod—New Zealand Olympian, bronze 1500 meter medalist at Munich Olympics, and New York City Marathon champ in 1983. 34, 72, 93, 97, 123-4, 131, 154, 187, 199, 214, 246, 254, 278, 285

DOHERTY, Ken—Former college coach, Penn Relays director and noted author of training books in the 1960s. 58, 117, 124, 162, 201

DRAYTON, Jerome—Canadian marathoner, won Boston in 1977 and placed 6th in the Montreal Olympic Marathon. 94, 176, 184

DWYER, Fred—Marty Liquori's high school coach. 22

EDELEN, Buddy—The first American to break 2:20 for the marathon, Edelen set a world record for the event with a 2:14:28 in 1963. Injuries slowed his 1964 Olympic marathon, but he managed a 6th in 2:18:12. 56, 178, 205

EL GERROUJ, Hicham—Moroccan middle-distance great. WR holder for the 1500m (3:26.00), mile (3:43.13), and 2000m (4:44.79). 28, 136.

ELLIOTT, Herb—Never beaten in the mile in his entire career, Elliott ranks as one of the greatest middle-distance runners of all time. He won the 1960 Olympic 1500 in Rome in the record time of 3:35.6—nearly 3 seconds faster than runner-up Michel Jazy of France. Elliott won 44 races in a row between 1954 and 1960. *5, 54, 92, 105, 121, 132-3, 199-200, 216, 244, 265*

ELLIOTT, James "Jumbo"—Villanova's coach for 46 years, Elliott coached the likes of Delany, Liquori, Coghlan, Sydney Maree and many other world-class middle distance runners. *46, 50, 53, 80, 96*

ELLIOTT, Peter—English middle distance runner, Elliott emerged at the end of the Coe-Ovett-Cram era and won a silver medal in the 1500-meters at Seoul. *276, 280*

EYESTONE, Ed—Two-time U.S. Olympic Marathon team member, placed 13th at Barcelona. *142, 145, 152-3, 258*

FLEMING, Tom—Two-time runner-up at the Boston Marathon and two-time New York City Marathon champ, now a coach and running store owner in New Jersey. *71, 78, 86, 100, 188*

FORDYCE, Bruce—Multi-time winner of South Africa's famous ultra—the Comrades Marathon. *99*

FOSTER, Brendan—English runner and 1976 Olympic bronze medalist at 10,000 meters, Foster once set world records for 3000 meters (7:35.2) and 2 miles (8:13.7). *87-8, 128, 222*

FOSTER, Jack—New Zealand Olympic marathoner at Munich and Montreal, at the ages of 40 and 44! Foster also won a silver marathon medal in the 1974 Commonwealth Games contested in Christchurch in his homeland. *53, 88, 92*

GEBRSELASSIE, Haile—Ethiopian distance great. Set four world records at 5000m and three WRs at 10,000m between 1994 and 1998. Current WR holder at 5000m (12:39.36) and 10,000m (26:22.75). Set 2-mile record of 8:01.08 broken a month and a half later by Daniel Komen's first-ever sub-8 2M (7:58.61) in 1997. *28, 136*

GOMEZ, Rudolfo—One of the first elite Mexican road racers and marathoners, Gomez (2:09:33) placed 4 seconds behind Salazar in their 1982 NYC Marathon duel. 91, 218

GROVES, Harry—Longtime, colorful coach at Penn State, Groves worked with numerous standouts of the early 1970s. 122, 152

GULICK, Jim—Coach at North Penn High School, Lansdale, Pa. 47-8

HÄGG, Gunder—Swedish distance star of the World War II era, Hägg established seven world records in his career, including a 4:01.3 mile in 1945. In 1946 he was suspended from amateur competition (along with Arne Andersson) for professionalism. 126, 220, 257, 267, 270, 275

HALBERG, Murray—Winner of the Rome Olympic 5000 meters (13:43.4), the gritty Kiwi was the runner that Lydiard said got the most out of his modest amount of talent. 19, 54, 76, 83, 243, 272

HERITAGE, Doris Brown—One of the pioneers for U.S. women's distance running in the 1960-1970 era, Doris Brown won five world cross-country titles. She coaches at Seattle-Pacific University. 165, 170

HILL, Ron—One of Great Britain's most prolific runners, Hill won the 1970 Boston Marathon and finished 6th in the 1972 Olympic race. 84-5, 97-8, 150, 184, 186, 229, 268

HUNT, Thom—Standout American distance runner of the 80s. 100, 233

HUSSEIN, Ibrahim—Kenyan runner who won the NYC Marathon in 1987 and three Boston Marathon (1988, 1991, 1992) titles. The smooth-running Hussein was the first African runner to win Boston. 26, 69, 181

IBBOTSON, Derek—British miler, Olympian, and world record-setter (3:57.2 in 1957). 193, 230, 281

IGLOI, Mihaly—Hungarian coach who placed a great emphasis on interval training. Coached outstanding milers such as Laszlo Tabori and Istvan Rozsavolgyi. 54, 59, 60

IKANGAA, Juma—Tanzania's great marathon runner, Ikangaa won the New York City Marathon—but was forced to settle for three runner-up finishes at Boston. 78, 82, 86, 252

JENNINGS, Lynn—Three time World Cross-Country Champion, Jennings also landed an Olympic bronze for the U.S. in the 1992 Barcelona 10,000. 54, 57, 99, 143, 206

JIPCHO, Ben—Kenyan runner who set a fast pace in the Mexico City Olympic 1500 that was eventually won by Keino (over Ryun), Jipcho placed second to Keino in the 1972 Olympic steeplechase. 62, 268

JOHNSON, Brooks—Former Stanford coach and Olympic team coach, Johnson's coaching stresses that middle distance and even long distance runners need to pay more attention to developing sprint speed. 52, 95, 242

JOHNSON, Michael—American sprint star. WR holder in the 200m (19.32) and 400m (43.18). 260

JONES, Steve—Won the 1984 Chicago Marathon in a then world best of 2:08:05, then brought down his PR to 2:07:13 at Chicago in 1985. 22, 200, 252, 265

KARDONG, Don—A U.S. Olympian in 1976, Kardong placed a close fourth in the Montreal Olympic Marathon. Few in the running world have contributed to the sport on so many levels: Kardong was at the forefront when runners made the transition from amateur to professional ranks; directs the Lilac Bloomsday mega-race in Spokane, Washington; and, is considered one of the best (and most humorous) writers on running—including *Thirty Phone Booths To Boston* (Macmillan, 1979). 21, 65, 68, 70-1, 81, 98, 148, 272

KEINO, Kipchoge—One of Kenya's first great runners, Keino competed in Tokyo, Mexico City and Munich. He beat Jim Ryun to win the 1500 meter gold in 1968 and—in addition to a 1500 silver—won the 3000-meter steeplechase gold at Munich in 1972. 118, 210, 274

KELLEY, John A. "Old John"—Won the Boston Marathon in 1935 and 1945 and finished second 7 times. Kelley was still finishing Boston when he was in his 80's. 70, 259, 286

KELLEY, John J. "Young John"—Won the Boston Marathon in 1957, the first American to win it in an 11-year span. No relation to "Old John." 82, 182, 185, 206, 258

KEMPAINEN, Bob—U.S. Olympic marathoner in Barcelona, Kempainen ran the fastest marathon ever by an American at the 1994 Boston Marathon when he placed 7th in 2:08:47. Kempainen also broke Pat Porter's 8-title streak when he won the 1990 U.S. Cross-Country crown. 72, 89, 204

KRISTIANSEN, Ingrid—Norway's Kristiansen is the only runner ever, male or female, to simultaneously hold world records in the 5000, 10,000 and the marathon. But her best Olympic finish was fourth in the marathon at Los Angeles. 134

KUSCSIK, Nina—First official women's champ with her 1972 Boston Marathon win, Kuscsik was a two-time NYC Marathon champ. 159, 164, 169, 172

LANDY, John—The second man to break the 4-minute mile barrier, Australia's "Gentleman John" brought the world record down to 3:57.9 less than two months later in Finland. Landy won a 1500-meter bronze medal in the 1956 Melbourne Games. 50, 113-4, 192, 195, 221

LEBOW, Fred—New York Road Runner's president who died in 1994, Lebow promoted big-time mega-marathoning at the helm of the NYC Marathon. 32, 135, 176, 186

LEITH, Jerry—Runner. 208

LIQUORI, Marty—Liquori won the famous "Dream Mile" against Jim Ryun at Franklin Field in 1971 to cap a brilliant career at Villanova. He also set a 5000 meter American record, but injuries and bad luck limited his Olympic appearances to Mexico City. 22, 55, 80, 84, 96, 99, 118, 119, 239, 269

LOPES, Carlos—Portugal's gold medal winner in the Los Angeles Olympic Games with a 2:09:21 at age 37. Lopes also set a world marathon record in 1985, won three World Cross-Country titles, and notched a silver in the 1976 Olympic 10,000 behind Lasse Viren. 66, 83, 115, 249

LOVELOCK, Jack—The 1936 Olympic 1500 meter champion from New Zealand, Lovelock also set a world record for the mile (4:07) during his career. 108, 115, 123, 129, 133-4, 238, 265, 267, 276, 284

LYDIARD, Arthur—New Zealand's most famous coach, Lydiard's trademark approach (base-building, hill phases and bounding drills) to middle and long distance running still holds great sway in modern training circles. Snell and Halberg were his most famous Olympic runners. 33, 46, 50, 54, 57, 61, 76, 83, 87, 122, 124, 151, 162, 205, 214-5

MARTIN, David—sports physiologist, 172

MASTERKOVA, Svetlana—Russian middle-distance great. 28

MENANDER—Ancient Greek playwright. 236, 240

MIDDLEMAN, Dan-1996 U.S. Olympian, and author of *Pain*, a running novel. 109

MILLS, Billy—Born on a Sioux Indian reservation in South Dakota, Mills's Olympic story is the stuff legends are made of. He won the 1964 Tokyo Olympic 10,000 meters with a 46-second PR and a heroic homestretch gallop. Mills also set a 6-mile world record in 1965. 117-8, 204, 212, 253, 277, 281

MIMOUN, Alain—Algerian-born French distance runner who often placed second to Zatopek. Mimoun won the 1956 Olympic Marathon. 222, 243

MOLLER, Lorraine—Native New Zealander, Olympic Marathon bronze medal winner at Barcelona and 1984 Boston Marathon champ. 167, 201, 234

MORCELI, Noureddine—Algerian middle-distance great. Set WRs at 1500m (twice), the mile, 2000m, and 3000m in the early to mid-90s. 216

MOORE, Kenny—Like Kardong, a man who has given much to the

sport of running at several different levels. A two-time Olympic marathoner ('68 and '72), the former University of Oregon runner placed fourth in the Munich Games. Many of his articles written for *Sports Illustrated* over the years are regarded as some of the best ever on running. Moore appeared in the 1982 movie *Personal Best.* 7, 27, 51, 79, 91, 93, 107, 178, 186, 188, 202, 250, 279

MOTA, Rosa—Portugal's Mota won a bronze medal at the L.A. Olympic Marathon, then struck gold at Seoul. She also won the Boston Marathon three times. 169

MUSSABINI, Sam—Professional sprint coach, Mussabini coached Olympic champion Harold Abrahams of Great Britian to the 100-meter gold at Paris in 1924—as depicted in n the running film classic *Chariots of Fire.* 46, 52, 53

NAKAMURA, Kiyoshi—Japanese coach of Seko and Wakiihuri, stern taskmaster Nakamura died in 1984 in a drowning accident rumored by some to have been a ritual suicide to atone for Seko's Olympic "failure" in 1984. 46, 55, 59, 61

NESBIT, Joan—World-class distance runner. 172

NEWTON, Arthur—South African ultra-distance runner and 4-time Comrades winner in the 1920s and 1930s. 116

NURMI, Paavo—The greatest of the "Flying Finns," Nurmi won 9 Olympic gold medals in distance running. There's a statue of him outside Helsinki Stadium and his likeness is on the Finnish 10-Mark currency note. 12, 52, 70, 95, 200, 210, 214, 220

THE OLYMPIAN, by Brian Glanville (129, 231, 255, 263, 280), and *ONCE A RUNNER,* by John L. Parker (64, 68, 194, 277)—Cult novels for competitive runners. Both published by Cedarwinds Publishing Company, 1-800-548-2388.

ONDIEKI, Lisa—Native of Australia, winner of the silver medal in the Seoul Olympic Marathon and 1992 champion of the New York City Marathon. 203

O'SULLIVAN, Marcus—Great Irish miler. 207

O'SULLIVAN, Sonia—Former Villanova star, the Irish Olympian won a gold medal over 3000 meters in the 1994 European Championships and set a world record for the rarely-run 2000 meters. 68, 170

OVETT, Steve—The Olympic gold medalist for 800 meters in 1980, the English middle distance star—rival of Coe and Cram—once set 1500 and mile world records. 61, 92, 152, 154, 211, 215

PAWALAK, Kim—American distance runner. 268

PEREC, Marie-Jose—French 400m star. 109

PFITZINGER, Pete—Two-time U.S. Olympic marathoner, Pfitzinger placed 11th (2:13:53) at Los Angeles in 1984. 87, 180

PIPPIG, Uta—Former East German runner now living and training in Boulder, Colorado, Pippig has twice won the Boston Marathon ('94 and '95) and the New York City Marathon ('93). With a lifetime PR of 2:21:45, she's gunning for the first sub-2:20 marathon effort for women. 23, 80, 112, 135, 159, 166, 179

PIRIE, Gordon—British distance star of the 1950s, Pirie won an Olympic silver in the Melbourne Olympic 5000. 105, 145, 166, 251, 283

PORTER, Pat—Eight-time winner of the U.S. Cross-Country Championships from 1982 through 1989. 24, 220

PREFONTAINE, Steve—Former University of Oregon great, Pre placed a gutsy fourth in the Olympic 5000 meters in Munich in 1972. Died in a car crash in 1975. 23, 62, 112, 117, 136, 202, 220, 238, 254, 275

ROBINSON, Roger—New Zealand writer (author of *Heroes and Sparrows*, Robinson has won masters division titles at both the Boston and New York Marathons. 74, 100, 171

RODGERS, Bill—Rodgers won four Boston and four New York City marathons in his heyday—and a slew of shorter road races on the U.S. circuit. The "King of the Roads" is still racing well in the masters division. 65, 116, 118, 175, 182, 186, 220, 232, 251, 253-4

ROELANTS, Gaston—Belgian distance star, Roelants won the gold medal in the 1964 Olympic steeplechase, and four international championships in cross-country. 102-4, 244, 250

RONO, Henry—In 1978, Kenya's Rono set four world records: 3000, 5000 and 10,000 meters, plus the 3000 meter steeplechase. 131, 270

RUNYAN, Marla—legally blind American Olympian at 1500m. 196

RYUN, Jim—A prodigious talent even as a teenager, Ryun set world records for the half-mile, 1500-meters and the mile. Finished second to Kenya's Kip Keino in the 1968 Olympic 1500 final in high-altitude Mexico City. Ryun was tripped in a trial heat at the Munich Games in '72 and never got a chance to strike Olympic gold. 22, 80, 127, 136, 194, 239

SAMUELSON, Joan Benoit—Winner of the historic first Olympic Marathon for women at Los Angeles in 1984 in 2:24:52. Maine-native Samuelson also won two Boston Marathons, including what was then a world-best of 2:22:43 in 1983. She defeated Norway's Ingrid Kristiansen in their 1985 Chicago Marathon showdown with a 2:21:21. 21, 26, 69, 134, 158, 188, 218

SALAZAR, Alberto—Cuban-born University of Oregon grad won three New York City titles and won the famous 1981 Boston "duel in the sun" with Dick Beardsley. 61, 112, 177, 219, 220, 225-6

SEGAL, Erich—American writer, runner. 176

SEKO, Toshihiko—Two-time Boston Marathon winner and one of Japan's greatest marathon runners, Seko placed sixth in the Los Angeles Olympic Marathon in 1984. 55, 61, 86

SHAKESPEARE—17, 29, 63, 75, 128, 137, 209, 223, 261

SHEEHAN, Dr. George—Author of *Running and Being,* among many other works. An leader in the U.S. running boom. 33, 74, 93, 177, 231

SHORTER, Frank—His 1972 gold medal marathon win at Munich is often credited with launching the "running boom" in the United States. Shorter also landed a silver medal in the Olympic marathon in 1976. 69, 108, 151, 175, 178, 180, 188, 194, 203, 212, 253, 262, 269, 272

SHRUBB, Alfred—English runner who won 20 British Championships between 1900 and 1920, Shrubb was one of the first to record his training methods in book form. 67, 72-3, 80, 88, 99, 120-2

SINCLAIR, Jon—U.S. road racer, major career wins at Peachtree and Bloomsday. 256, 281

SNELL, Peter—Won the 800 meter gold at Rome in Olympic record time (1:46.3), then struck "double" gold at Tokyo in 1964 with victories in the 1500 and 800—breaking his own Olympic record in the latter event with a 1:45.1. 54-5, 83, 118-9

SPIVEY, Jim—U.S. Olympian and a 3:50.5 miler. 207

SQUIRES, Bill—Distance running coach, Squires worked with Bill Rodgers and others on the Boston running scene. 61, 93, 219

STAMPFL, Franz—Austrian-born professional coach, Stampfl worked with runners in England and Australia. He helped set up Bannister's sub-4 minute mile attempt in 1954 and later coached Australian Ralph Doubell's 1968 Olympic 800 meter win at Mexico City. 56-7, 59, 109

STEFFNEY, Manfred—German coach. 172

STERN, Marty—Coached Villanova women to five straight NCAA Cross-Country titles from 1990 to 1994 and numerous Penn Relays victories. 52, 56, 58, 99, 154

STEWART, Jason—U.S. Army captain and runner. 195

SWITZER, Kathrine—After her famous 1967 "K. Switzer" entry in the then men-only Boston Marathon, Switzer—race commentator and promoter—pushed for a women's Olympic Marathon. 159, 164, 167-9, 171

TEGEN, Peter—Coach at the University of Wisconsin. 96

THOMAS, Albie—Cerutty-coached Australian runner of the late-1950s /early-1960s era, the diminutive but tough Thomas set world records over two miles (8:32) and three-miles (13:10.8). 51, 130

TREACY, John—One of Ireland's greatest runners, Treacy won the silver medal in the Los Angeles Olympic Marathon. Treacy also won two World Cross-Country titles in 1978 and 1979. 78, 104, 144, 217, 259

TRAUTMANN, John—Former Georgetown star, U.S. road and track racer. 116

VÄÄTÄINEN, Juha—Finnish star nicknamed "Juha the Cruel," he won both the 5000 and 10,000 meter races in the 1971 European Championships. 26, 91, 141, 221, 229

VASALA, Pekka—Finnish middle-distance runner. Vasala won the Olympic 1500 meters at Munich in 1972 (3:36.3), outkicking defending champ Kip Keino. 153, 222

VIREN, Lasse—Finland's four-time Olympic gold medalist—the "double-double" of 5000 and 10,000 meters (1972 and 1976). Viren's greatest win may have been the '72 10,000 at Munich, when he fell at mid-race, but got up and charged back to victory—in addition to breaking Ron Clarke's 7-year-old world record by 1 second in 27:38.4. Some critics have accused Viren of "blood boosting"—a practice he denied and was also not against the Olympic rules during his career. 46, 52, 74, 85, 119, 128, 133, 214, 215, 230, 237, 243, 255, 268

WAITZ, Grete—Norwegian great who began her career as a middle distance runner, then moved up to win the New York City Marathon nine times. Waitz won five World Cross-Country titles. She also won the silver medal in the L.A. Olympic Marathon in 1984. 22, 107, 168, 182, 187, 188, 203, 210

WAKIIHURI, Douglas—Kenyan racer who trained in Japan under Nakamura, he won a silver medal in the Seoul Olympic Marathon. 59, 179, 217, 222

WALKER, John—First man to break 3:50 for the mile, the popular New Zealander also won the 1976 Olympic 1500. 90, 123, 128, 131-2, 194-5, 216, 244, 257

WARDLAW, Chris—Australian marathoner and two-time Olympian (1976 and 1980). 7, 26, 201, 239

WEBB, Alan—Set the U.S. high school mile record (3:53.43) in 2001, breaking Jim Ryun's long-standing mark. 127, 136

WELCH, Priscilla—British marathoner Welch was a former smoker who didn't begin to train seriously until her mid-30s. At the age of 39 she placed 6th in the L.A. Olympic Marathon and three years later won the New York City Marathon in 2:30:17. 21

WILLIAMS, Todd—U.S. Olympian in the 10,000 meters at Barcelona in '92, Williams won the U.S. Cross-Country title in 1991. 98, 204, 234

WINFREY, Oprah—Talk-show host, TV producer, magazine editor, runner. Inspired millions with her run in the 1994 Marine Corps Marathons. 37, 181

WOHLHUTER, Rick—U.S. middle-distance standout, bronze medalist at 1976 Olympic 800 meters. 240-1

YIFTER, Miruts—Known as "Yifter the Shifter" because of his killer kick, the Ethiopian won golds for both the 5000 and 10,000 meter races at Moscow in 1980. 122, 219, 221

YOUNG, George—U.S. distance runner. Young won a bronze medal in the steeplechase at the 1968 Olympics. 79, 181

ZATOPEK, Emil—Czech Olympic great; winner of 4 gold medals, including 1952 "triple" at Helsinki where he won the 5,000 meters, 10,000 meters and the marathon—all three in Olympic record time. 12, 13, 20, 68, 71, 83, 90, 92, 133, 161, 168, 176, 179, 183, 198, 210, 217, 221, 228, 232, 241, 255, 259, 280, 283, 285

THE RUNNING TRIVIA BOOK: 1001 Questions from the Sprints to the Marathon. By Mark Will-Weber. "An often funny, always fascinating history of running that's merely disguised as a parlor game." —*Runner's World* 304 pages, hardcover, $22. ISBN 1-891369-57-1

AMERICAN MILER: The Life and Times of Glenn Cunningham. The incredible story of a boy whose legs were terrible burned at age seven, who then grew up to be world record holder in the mile. 432 pages, $15, paperback. ISBN: 1-891369-59-8

RACING FOR RECOVERY: From Addict to Ironman. Todd Crandell's inspiring story of transforming himself from a drug-addicted alcoholic mess to a healthy, driven athlete. 192 pages, paperback, $14. ISBN: 1-891369-61-X.

TRAINING FOR MORTALS: John Bingham and Coach Jenny Hadfield's extremely popular running log. 160 pages, spiral bound, $14.95, ISBN: 978-1-891369-69-8.

THE THRILL OF VICTORY, THE AGONY OF MY FEET: Tales from the World of Adventure Racing. Running, climbing, paddling, cycling, and crawling through the worst spots on earth-the joys of adventure racing, as told by a full range of competitors, from novice to professional. $14, paperback, 328 pages, ISBN: 1-891369-54-7.

THE RUNNER'S HIGH: Illumination and Ecstasy in Motion. True stories of running's most exalted moments—the joy and awe and transcendence it can bring. 256 pages, paperback, $14, ISBN: 1-891369-49-0

GOD ON THE STARTING LINE: The Triumph of a Catholic School Running Team and Its Jewish Coach, by Marc Bloom "A classic, a tribute to all those who pursue excellence with talent, pride, courage, and the ability to endure." —Bud Greenspan. 240 pages, paperback, $14, ISBN: 978-1-891369-74-2

THE GREATEST: The Haile Gebrselassie Story. Two Olympic 10,000m golds; 8 world championships indoors and outdoors; 17 world records over four different distances; a fifty-four race winning streak—Haile Gebrselassie utterly dominated a decade of distance running. 288 pages, paperback, $14, ISBN: 1-891369-48-2.

HOW RUNNING CHANGED MY LIFE: True Stories of the Power of Running. 43 moving personal stories about the power of running to elevate, improve, and inspire us. Paperback, 208 pages, $15. ISBN: 1-891369-30-X.

RUNNING IN LITERATURE: A Guide for Scholars, Readers, Runners, Joggers, and Dreamers. By Roger Robinson. A brilliant, readable, funny book. "Every page is a treasure trove." —Amby Burfoot. 304 pages, hardcover, $22, ISBN: 1-891369-41-5.

ZENDURANCE: A Spiritual Guide for Endurance Athletes. By Shane Alton Eversfield. Foreword by Paula Newby-Fraser, 8-time World Ironman Champion. Using some simple Zen techniques to remove the obstacles to attaining "effortless power." A fascinating book for athletes of all abilities. 328 pages, paperback, $20. ISBN: 1-891369-43-1.